THE ART OF
LAWN TENNIS

WILLIAM T. TILDEN

WILLIAM T. TILDEN
 Champion of the world, in action.

THE ART OF
LAWN TENNIS

BY

WILLIAM T. TILDEN 2ᴰ
CHAMPION OF THE WORLD

ILLUSTRATED

Fredonia Books
Amsterdam, The Netherlands

The Art of Lawn Tennis

by
William T. Tilden

ISBN: 1-58963-332-6

Reprinted from the 1922 edition

Fredonia Books
Amsterdam, The Netherlands
http://www.fredoniabooks.com

In order to make original editions of historical works available to scholars at an economical price, this facsimile of the original edition of 1922 is reproduced from the best available copy and has been digitally enhanced to improve legibility, but the text remains unaltered to retain historical authenticity.

To
R. D. K.
AND
M. W. J.
MY "BUDDIES

W. T. T. 2D

INTRODUCTION

TENNIS is at once an art and a science. The game as played by such men as Norman E. Brookes, the late Anthony Wilding, William M. Johnston, and R. N. Williams is art. Yet like all true art, it has its basis in scientific methods that must be learned and learned thoroughly for a foundation before the artistic structure of a great tennis game can be constructed.

Every player who helps to attain a high degree of efficiency should have a clearly defined method of development and adhere to it. He should be certain that it is based on sound principles and, once assured of that, follow it, even though his progress seems slow and discouraging.

I began tennis wrong. My strokes were wrong and my viewpoint clouded. I had no early training such as many of our American boys have at the present time. No one told me the importance of the fundamentals of the game, such as keeping the eye on the ball or correct body position and footwork. I was given a racquet and allowed to hit the ball. Naturally, like all beginners, I acquired many very serious faults. I worried along with moderate success until I had been graduated from school, beating some fairly good players, but losing some matches to men below my class. The year following my graduation the new Captain of my Alma Mater's team asked me if I would aid him in developing the squad for next year. Well, "Fools rush in where angels fear to tread," so I said Yes.

At that point my tennis education began.

The youngsters comprising our tennis squad all knew me well and felt at perfect liberty to ask me as many questions as they could think up. I was besieged with requests to explain why Jones missed a forehand drive down the side-line, or Smith couldn't serve well, or Brown failed to hit the ball at all. Frankly, I did not know, but I answered them something at the moment and said to myself it was time I learned some fundamentals of tennis. So I began to study the reasons why certain shots are missed and others made. Why certain balls are hit so much faster though with less effort than others, and why some players are great while most are only good. I am still studying, but my results to date have resulted in a definite system to be learned, and it is this which I hope to explain to you in my book.

Tennis has a language all its own. The idioms of the game should be learned, as all books on the game are written in tennis parlance. The technical terms and their counterpart in slang need to be understood to thoroughly grasp the idea in any written tennis account.

I do not believe in using a great deal of space

carefully defining each blade of grass on a court, or each rule of the game. It gets nowhere. I do advocate teaching the terms of the game.

1. THE COURT.

The Base-line=The back line.

The Service-line=The back line of the service court, extending from side-line to side-line at a point 21 feet from the net.

The Alleys=The space on each side of the court between the side service-line and the outside side-line of a doubles court. They are used only when playing doubles and are not marked on a single court.

The Net=The barrier that stretches across the court in the exact centre. It is 3 feet high at the centre and 3 feet 6 inches high at the posts which stand 3 feet outside the side-lines.

2. STROKES (Two General Classes).

A. Ground strokes=All shots hit from the base-lines off the bounce of the ball.

B. Volleys=Shots hit while the ball is in flight through the air, previous to its bound.

The Service=The method of putting the ball in play.

The Drive=A ground stroke hit with a flat racquet face and carrying top spin.

The Chop=An undercut ground stroke is the general definition of a chop. The slice and chop are so closely related that, except in stroke analysis, they may be called chop.

Stop Volley=Blocking a ball short in its flight.

Half Volley or Trap Shot=A pick up.

The Smash=Hitting on the full any overhead ball.

The Lob=Hitting the ball in a high parabola.

3. TWIST ON THE BALL.

Top Spin=The ball spins towards the ground and in the direction of its flight.

Chop, Cut, or Drag=The ball spins upwards from the ground and against the line of flight. This is slightly deviated in the slice, but all these terms are used to designate the under-struck, back-spinning ball.

Reverse Twist=A ball that carries a rotary spin that curves one way and bounces the opposite.

Break=A spin which causes the ball to bounce at an angle to its line of flight.

4. LET=A service that touches the net in its flight yet falls in court, or any illegal or irregular point that does not count.

5. FAULT=An illegal service.

6. OUT=Any shot hit outside legal boundaries of the court.

7. GOOD=Any shot that strikes in a legal manner prescribed by rules of the game.

8. FOOTFAULT=An illegal service delivery due to incorrect position of the server's feet.

9. SERVER=Player delivering service.

10. RECEIVER or STRIKER=Player returning service.

W. T. T.

WIMBLEDON, *July* 1920

PREFACE TO NEW EDITION

The season of 1921 was so epoch-making in the game of tennis, combining as it did the greatest number of Davis Cup matches that have ever been held in one year, the invasion of France and England by an American team, the first appearance in America of Mlle. Suzanne Lenglen and her unfortunate collapse, and finally the rise to prominence of Japan as a leading factor in the tennis world that I have incorporated a record of the season's outstanding features and some sidelights and personality sketches on the new stars in the new addition of this book.

The importance of women's tennis has grown so tremendously in the past few years that I have also added a review of the game and its progress in America. Not only has Mlle. Lenglen placed her mark indelibly on the pages of tennis history but 1921 served to raise Mrs. Molla Bjurstedt Mallory to the position in the world that she rightly deserves, that of the greatest match winner of all women. The past season brought the return to American courts of Mrs. May Sutton Bundy and Miss Mary Browne, in itself an event of sufficient importance to set the year apart as one of highest value.

The outstanding preformances of the two juniors, Vincent Richards and Arnold Jones, must be regarded as worthy of permanent recognition and among the outstanding features of a noteworthy year. Thus it is with a sense of recording history-making facts that I turn to the events of 1921.

WILLIAM T. TILDEN 2D

GERMANTOWN,
    PHILADELPHIA

CONTENTS

PART IV: SOME SIDELIGHTS ON FAMOUS PLAYERS

ILLUSTRATIONS

ILLUSTRATIONS

PAGE

BURN, *America,* 1921. M. E. Mc-
LOUGHLIN AND T. C. BUNDY, *America,* 1914 84

XI FAMOUS DAVIS CUP STARS. NORMAN E.
BROOKES, *Australia.* ANTHONY F.
WILDING, *New Zealand.* BEALS
WRIGHT, *America.* W. A. LARNED,
America 85

XII THE 1921 AUSTRALIAN DAVIS CUP TEAM.
J. O. ANDERSON, J. B. HAWKES, NOR-
MAN PEACH AND C. V. TODD.
THE 1920 AMERICAN DAVIS CUP TEAM.
R. N. WILLIAMS 2ND, W. M. JOHN-
STON, CAPTAIN SAMUEL HARDY, WM.
T. TILDEN 2ND AND C. S. GARLAND 93

XIII FORMER CHAMPIONS OF AMERICA. R. NOR-
RIS WILLIAMS. WILLIAM M. JOHN-
STON. MAURICE E. McLOUGHLIN.
ROBERT LINDLEY MURRAY . . . 108

XIV AN ECHO OF THE WAR. JULIAN S. MYRICK,
WALTER CAMP, E. F. TORREY AND
R. L. MURRAY
DAVIS CUP DOUBLES TEAM 1913. M. E.
McLOUGHLIN AND H. H. HACKETT.
FRIENDLY ENEMIES. ICHIYA KUMAGAE
AND VINCENT RICHARDS 124

XV WALLACE F. JOHNSTON, *America.* S.
HOWARD VOSHELL, *America.* ICHIYA
KUMAGAE, *Japan.* WATSON M.
WASHBURN, *America* 140

PART I: TENNIS TECHNIQUE—STROKES AND FUNDAMENTALS OF THE GAME

THE ART OF LAWN TENNIS

PART I: TENNIS TECHNIQUE—STROKES AND FUNDAMENTALS OF THE GAME

CHAPTER I

FOR NOVICES ONLY

I TRUST this initial effort of mine in the world of letters will find a place among both novices and experts in the tennis world. I am striving to interest the student of the game by a somewhat prolonged discussion of match play, which I trust will shed a new light on the game.

May I turn to the novice at my opening and speak of certain matters which are second nature to the skilled player?

The best tennis equipment is not too good for the beginner who seeks really to succeed. It is a saving in the end, as good quality material so far outlasts poor.

Always dress in tennis clothes when engaging in tennis. White is the established colour. Soft shirt, white flannel trousers, heavy white socks, and rubber-soled shoes form the accepted dress for tennis. Do not appear on the courts in dark clothes, as they are apt to be heavy and hinder your speed of movement, and also they are a violation of the unwritten ethics of the game.

The question of choosing a racquet is a much more serious matter. I do not advocate forcing a certain racquet upon any player. All the standard makes are excellent. It is in weight, balance, and size of handle that the real value of a racquet frame depends, while good stringing is essential to obtain the best results.

The average player should use a racquet that weighs between 13½ and 14½ ounces inclusive. I think that the best results may be obtained by a balance that is almost even or slightly heavy on the head. Decide your handle from the individual choice. Pick the one that fits comfortably in the hand. Do not use too small a handle or too light a racquet, as it is apt to turn in the hand. I recommend a handle of 5¼ to 5⅜ inches at the grip. Do not use a racquet you do not like merely because your best friend advises it. It may suit him perfectly, but would not do for you at all. Do not start children playing tennis with an under-sized racquet. It weakens the wrist and does not aid the child in learning strokes. Start a child, boy or girl, with a full-sized racquet of at least 13 ounces.

After you have acquired your racquet, make a firm resolve to use good tennis balls, as a regular bounce is a great aid to advancement, while a "dead" ball is no practice at all.

If you really desire to succeed at the game and advance rapidly, I strongly urge you to see all the good tennis you can. Study the play of the leading players and strive to copy their strokes. Read all the tennis instruction books you can find. They are a great assistance. I shall be accused of "press-agitating" my own book by this statement, but such was my belief long before I ever thought of writing a book of my own.

More tennis can be learned off the court, in the study of theory, and in watching the best players in action, than can ever be learned in actual play. I do not mean miss opportunities to play. Far from it. Play whenever possible, but strive when playing to put in practice the theories you have read or the strokes you have watched.

Never be discouraged at slow progress. The trick over some stroke you have worked over for weeks unsuccessfully will suddenly come to you when least expected. Tennis players are the product of hard work. Very few are born geniuses at the game.

Tennis is a game that pays you dividends all your life. A tennis racquet is a letter of introduction in any town. The brotherhood of the game is universal, for none but a good sportsman can succeed in the game for any lengthy period. Tennis provides relaxation, excitement, exercise, and pure enjoyment to the man who is tied hard and fast to his business until late afternoon. Age is not a drawback. Vincent Richards held the National Doubles Championship of America at fifteen, while William A. Larned won the singles at past forty. Men of sixty are seen daily on the clubs' courts of England and America enjoying their game as keenly as any boy. It is to this game, in great measure, that they owe the physical fitness which enables them to play at their advanced age.

The tennis players of the world wrote a magnificent page in the history of the World War. No branch of sport sent more men to the colours from every country in the world than tennis, and these men returned with glory or paid the supreme sacrifice on the field of honour.

I transgressed from my opening to show you that tennis is a game worth playing and playing well. It deserves your best, and only by learning it correctly can you give that best.

If in my book I help you on your way to fame, I feel amply repaid for all the time spent in analysing the strokes and tactics I set before you in these pages.

I am going to commence my explanation by talking to the players whose games are not yet formed. At least once every season I go back to first principles to pull myself out of some rut into which carelessness dropped me.

From a long and, many times, sad experience over a period of some ten years of tournament tennis, I believe the following order of development produces the quickest and most lasting results:

1. Concentration on the game.
2. Keep the eye on the ball.
3. Foot-work and weight-control.
4. Strokes.
5. Court position.
6. Court generalship or match play.
7. Tennis psychology.

Tennis is a game of intimate personal relation. You constantly find yourself meeting some definite idea of your opponent. The personal equation is the basis of tennis success. A great player not only knows himself, in both strength and weakness, but he must study his opponent at all times. In order to be able to do this a player must not be hampered by a glaring weakness in the fundamentals of his own game, or he will be so occupied trying to hide it that he will have no time to worry his opponent. The fundamental weakness of Gerald Patterson's backhand stroke is so apparent that any player within his class dwarfs Patterson's style by continually pounding at it. The Patterson overhead and service are first class, yet both are rendered impotent, once a man has solved the method of returning low to the backhand, for Patterson seldom succeeds in taking the offensive again in that point.

I am trying to make clear the importance of such first principles as I will now explain.

CONCENTRATION

Tennis is played primarily with the mind. The most perfect racquet technique in the world will not suffice if the directing mind is wandering. There are many causes of a wandering mind in a tennis match. The chief one is lack of interest in the game. No one should play tennis with an idea of real success unless he cares sufficiently about the game to be willing to do the drudgery necessary in learning the game correctly. Give it up at once unless you are willing to work. Conditions of play or the noises in the gallery often confuse and bewilder experienced match-players playing under new surroundings. Complete concentration on the matter in hand is the only cure for a wandering mind, and the sooner the lesson is learned the more rapid the improvement of the player. An amusing example, to all but the player affected, occurred at the finals of the Deleware State Singles Championship at Wilmington. I was playing Joseph J. Armstrong. The Championship Court borders the No. 1 hole of the famous golf course. The score stood at one set all and 3–4 and 30–40, Armstrong serving. He served a fault and started a second delivery. Just as he commenced his swing, a loud and very lusty "Fore!" rang out from the links. Armstrong unconsciously looked away and served his delivery to the backstop and the game to me. The umpire refused to "let" call and the incident closed.

Yet a wandering mind in that case meant the loss of a set.

The surest way to hold a match in mind is to play for every set, every game in the set, every point in the game and, finally, every shot in the point. A set is merely a conglomeration of made and missed shots, and the man who does not miss is the ultimate victor.

Please do not think I am advocating "pat-ball." I am not. I believe in playing for your shot every time you have an opening. I do not believe in trying to win the point every time you hit the ball. Never allow your concentration on any game to become so great that you do not at all times know the score and play to it. I mean both point score and game score. In my explanation of match play in a later chapter I am going into a detailed account of playing to the score. It is as vital in tennis as it is in bridge, and all bridge players know that the score is the determining factor in your mode of bidding. Let me urge again concentration. Practise seriously. Do not fool on the court, as it is the worst enemy to progress. Carelessness or laziness only results in retrogression, never progress.

Let me turn now to the first principle of all ball games, whether tennis, golf, cricket, baseball, polo, or football.

KEEP YOUR EYE ON THE BALL!

Just a few statistics to show you how vital it is that the eye must be kept on the ball *until the moment of striking it.*

About 85 per cent of the points in tennis are errors, and the remainder earned points. As the standard of play rises the percentage of errors drops until, in the average high-class tournament match, 60 per cent are errors and 40 per cent aces. Any average superior to this is super-tennis.

Thus the importance of getting the ball in play cannot be too greatly emphasized. Every time you put the ball back to your opponent you give him another chance to miss.

There are several causes for missing strokes. First, and by far the largest class, is not looking at the ball up to the moment of striking it. Fully 80 per cent of all errors are caused by taking the eye from the ball in the last one-fifth of a second of its flight. The remaining 20 per cent of errors are about 15 per cent bad footwork, and the other 5 per cent poor racquet work and bad bounces.

The eye is a small camera. All of us enjoy dabbling in amateur photography, and every amateur must take "action" pictures with his first camera. It is a natural desire to attain to the hardest before understanding how to reach it. The result is one of two things: either a blurred moving object and a clear background, or a clear moving object and a blurred background. Both suggest speed, but only one is a good picture of the object one attempted to photograph. In the first case the camera eye was focused on the background and not on the object, while in the second, which produced the result desired, the camera eye was firmly focused on the moving object itself. Just so with the human eye. It will give both effects, but never a clear background and moving object at the same time, once that object reaches a point 10 feet from the eye. The perspective is wrong, and the eye cannot adjust itself to the distance range speedily enough.

Now the tennis ball is your moving object while the court, gallery, net, and your opponent constitute your background. You desire to hit the ball cleanly, therefore do not look at the other factors concerned, but concentrate solely on focusing the eye firmly on the ball, and watching it until the moment of impact with your racquet face.

"How do I know where my opponent is, or how much court I have to hit in?" ask countless beginners.

Remember this: that a tennis court is always the same size, with the net the same height and in the same relation to you at all times, so there is no need to look at it every moment or so to see if it has moved. Only an earthquake can change its position. As to your opponent, it makes little difference about his position, because it is determined by the shot you are striving to return. Where he will be I will strive to explain in my chapter on court position; but his whereabouts are known without looking at him. You are not trying to hit him. You strive to miss him. Therefore, since you must watch what you strive to hit and not follow what you only wish to miss, keep your eye on the ball, and let your opponent take care of himself.

Science has proved that given a tennis ball passing from point A to point B with the receiving player at B, that if the player at B keeps his eye on the ball throughout its full flight his chance of making a good

$$A \quad 1 \quad 2 \quad 3 \quad 4 \quad B$$

return at B is five times as great as if he took his eye off the ball at a point 4, or $\frac{4}{5}$ of a second of its flight. Likewise it is ten times as great at B as it is if the eye is removed from the ball at 3, or $\frac{3}{5}$ of a second of its flight. Why increase your chances of error by five times or ten times when it is un-necessary?

The average player follows the ball to 4, and then he takes a last look at his opponent to see where he is, and by so doing increases his chance of error five times. He judges the flight of the ball some 10 feet away, and never really sees it again until he has hit it (if he does). A slight deflection caused by the wind or a small misjudgment of curve will certainly mean error. Remembering the 85 per cent errors in tennis, I again ask you if it is worth while to take the risk?

There are many other reasons why keeping the eye on the ball is a great aid to the player. It tends to hold his attention so that outside occurrences will not distract. Movements in the gallery are not seen, and stray dogs, that seem to particularly enjoy sleeping in the middle of a tennis court during a hard match, are not seen on their way to their sleeping quarters. Having learned the knack of watching

FOREHAND GRIP. FRONT VIEW
Notice the straight line of the arm, hand and racquet, the flat racquet face, the natural finger position on the handle. The racquet is in position to hit a forehand drive.

FOREHAND GRIP. BACK VIEW
The line is straight, the head of the racquet slightly in advance of the hand. This pose is at the moment of contact between ball and racquet.

THE COMPLETED SWING OF THE FOREHAND DRIVE

Notice the body position, at right angles to the net, the weight on the front or left foot, having passed from the right foot with the swing, just at the moment the ball is struck. The racquet is carried to the limit of the swing and falls into the left hand at height of the shoulder. The racquet face has passed over the ball. The reader is looking through the strings. The stroke was made with the far side of the racquet from the camera. The eye is following the ball in its flight. The whole movement is forward. The tendency in hitting a forehand is to stop the swing too soon. Notice the full follow through to the extreme limit of my swing. The hitting plane in this picture is too high, the shot having been made almost at the shoulder. The correct hitting plane for the forehand drive is along the line of the waist. Play all drives at this height if possible. Step back to allow the ball to fall waist high if necessary rather than play it at the shoulder. Hit your forehand drive decisively but do not attempt to kill every shot. Be accurate first and attain speed second.

the ball at all times, I felt that nothing would worry me, until three years ago at the American Championships, when I was playing T. R. Pell. A press-camera man eluded the watchful eye of the officials, and unobtrusively seated himself close to our side-line to acquire some action pictures. Pell angled sharply by to my backhand, and I ran at my hardest for the shot, eyes fixed solely on the ball. I hauled off to hit it a mighty drive, which would have prob-ably gone over the backstop, when suddenly I heard a camera click just under me, and the next moment camera, pressman, and tennis player were rolling in a heap all over the court. The pressman got his action picture and a sore foot where I walked on him, and all I got was a sore arm and a ruffled temper. That's why I don't like cameras right under my nose when I play matches, but for all that I still advocate keeping your eye on the ball.

GRIP, FOOTWORK, AND STROKES

Footwork is weight control. It is correct body position for strokes, and out of it all strokes should grow. In explaining the various forms of stroke and footwork I am writing as a right-hand player. Left-handers should simply reverse the feet.

Racquet grip is a very essential part of stroke, because a faulty grip will ruin the finest serving. There is the so-called Western or Californian grip as typified by Maurice E. M'Loughlin, Willis E. Davis, and, to a slightly modified degree, W. M.

Johnston, the American champion. It is a natural grip for a top forehand drive. It is inherently weak for the backhand, as the only natural shot is a chop stroke.

The English grip, with the low wrist on all ground strokes, has proved very successful in the past. Yet the broken line of the arm and hand does not commend itself to me, as any broken line is weak under stress.

The Eastern American grip, which I advocate, is the English grip without the low wrist and broken line. To acquire the forehand grip, hold the racquet with the edge of the frame towards the ground and the face perpendicular, the handle towards the body, and "shake hands" with it, just as if you were greeting a friend. The handle settled comfortably and naturally into the hand, the line of the arm, hand, and racquet are one. The swing brings the racquet head on a line with the arm, and the whole racquet is merely an extension of it.

The backhand grip is a quarter circle turn of hand on the handle, bringing the hand on top of the handle and the knuckles directly up. The shot travels *across* the wrist.

This is the best basis for a grip. I do not advocate learning this grip exactly, but model your natural grip as closely as possible on these lines without sacrificing your own comfort or individuality.

Having once settled the racquet in the hand, the next question is the position of the body and the order of developing strokes.

In explaining footwork I am, in future, going to refer in all forehand shots to the right foot as R or "back" foot, and to the left as L or "front." For the backhand the L foot is "back" and R is "front."

All tennis strokes should be made with the body at right angles to the net, with the shoulders lined up parallel to the line of flight of the ball. The weight should always travel forward. It should pass from the back foot to the front foot at the moment of striking the ball. Never allow the weight to be going away from the stroke. It is weight that determines the "pace" of a stroke; swing that decides the "speed."

Let me explain the definitions of "speed" and "pace." "Speed" is the actual rate with which a ball travels through the air. "Pace" is the momentum with which it comes off the ground. Pace is weight. It is the "sting" the ball carries when it comes off the ground, giving the inexperienced or unsuspecting player a shock of force which the stroke in no way showed.

Notable examples of "pace" are such men as W. A. Larned, A. W. Gore, J. C. Parke, and among the younger players, R. N. Williams, Major A. R. F. Kingscote, W. M. Johnston, and, on his forehand stroke, Charles S. Garland.

M. E. M'Loughlin, Willis E. Davis, Harold Throckmorton and several others are famous "speed" exponents.

A great many players have both "speed" and "pace." Some shots may carry both.

The order of learning strokes should be:

1. The Drive. Fore- and backhand. This is the foundation of all tennis, for you cannot build up a net attack unless you have the ground stroke to open the way. Nor can you meet a net attack successfully unless you can drive, as that is the only successful passing shot.

2. The Service.

3. The Volley and Overhead Smash.

4. The Chop or Half Volley and other incidental and ornamental strokes.

CHAPTER II

THE DRIVE

THE forehand drive is the opening of every offensive in tennis, and, as such, should be most carefully studied. There are certain rules of footwork that apply to all shots. To reach a ball that is a short distance away, advance the foot that is away from the shot and thus swing into position to hit. If a ball is too close to the body, retreat the foot closest to the shot and drop the weight back on it, thus, again, being in position for the stroke. When hurried, and it is not possible to change the foot position, throw the weight on the foot closest to the ball.

The receiver should always await the service facing the net, but once the serve is started on the way to court, the receiver should at once attain the position to receive it with the body at right angles to the net.

The forehand drive is made up of one continuous swing of the racquet that, for the purpose of analysis, may be divided into three parts:

1. The portion of the swing behind the body, which determines the speed of the stroke.

2. That portion immediately in front of the body

which determines the direction and, in conjunction with weight shift from one foot to the other, the pace of the shot.

3. The portion beyond the body, comparable to the golfer's "follow through," determines spin, top or slice, imparted to the ball.

All drives should be topped. The slice shot is a totally different stroke.

To drive straight down the side-line, construct in theory a parallelogram with two sides made up of the side-line and your shoulders, and the two ends, the lines of your feet, which should, if extended, form the right angles with the side-lines. Meet the ball at a point about 4 to 4½ feet from the body immediately in front of the belt buckle, and shift the weight from the back to the front foot at the *moment of striking the ball*. The swing of the racquet should be flat and straight through. The racquet head should be on a line with the hand, or, if anything, slightly in advance; the whole arm and the racquet should turn slightly over the ball as it leaves the racquet face and the stroke continue to the limit of the swing, thus imparting top spin to the ball.

The hitting plane for all ground strokes should be between the knees and shoulders. The most favourable plane is on a line with the waist.

In driving across the court from the right (or No. 1) court, advance the L or front foot slightly towards the side-line and shift the weight a fraction of a second sooner. As the weight shifts, pivot slightly on the L foot and drive flat, diagonally, across the court. Do not "pull" your cross-court drive, unless with the express purpose of passing the net man and using that method to disguise your shot.

Never step away from the ball in driving cross court. Always throw your weight in the shot.

The forehand drive from the No. 2 (or left) court is identically the same for the straight shot down your opponent's forehand. For the cross drive to his backhand, you must conceive of a diagonal line from your backhand corner to his, and thus make your stroke with the footwork as if this imaginary line were the side-line. In other words, line up your body along your shot and make your regular drive. Do not try to "spoon" the ball over with a delayed wrist motion, as it tends to slide the ball off your racquet.

All drives should be made with a stiff, locked wrist. There is no wrist movement in a true drive. Top spin is imparted by the arm, not the wrist.

The backhand drive follows closely the principles of the forehand, except that the weight shifts a moment sooner, and the R or front foot should always be advanced a trifle closer to the side-line than the L so as to bring the body clear of the swing. The ball should be met in front of the right leg, instead of the belt buckle, as the great tendency in backhand shots is to slice them out of the side-line, and this will pull the ball cross court, obviating this error. The racquet head must be slightly in advance of the hand to aid in bringing the ball in the court. Do not strive for too much top spin on your backhand.

I strongly urge that no one should ever favour one department of his game, in defence of a weakness. Develop both forehand and backhand, and do not "run around" your backhand, particularly in return of service. To do so merely opens your court. If you should do so, strive to ace your returns, because a weak effort would only result in a kill by your opponent.

Do not develop one favourite shot and play nothing but that. If you have a fair cross-court drive, do not use it in practice, but strive to develop an equally fine straight shot.

Remember that the fast shot is the straight shot. The cross drive must be slow, for it has not the room owing to the increased angle and height of the net. Pass down the line with your drive, but open the court with your cross-court shot.

Drives should have depth. The average drive should hit behind the service-line. A fine drive should hit within 3 feet of the base-line. A cross-court drive should be shorter than a straight drive, so as to increase the possible angle. Do not always play one length drive, but learn to vary your distance according to your man. You should drive deep against a base-liner, but short against a net player, striving to drop them at his feet as he comes in.

BACKHAND GRIP. FRONT VIEW

Note the hand on top of the racquet handle, yet retaining the straight line of arm, hand and racquet as in the forehand. The change from the forehand grip is one quarter circle of the handle. The knuckles are up and directly towards the opponent. The head of the racquet is advanced slightly towards the ball.

BACKHAND GRIP. BACK VIEW

Notice the line of arm and racquet is straight and the hand on top of the handle. The thumb in my stroke is around the handle, but may be placed up the handle if desired. Personally, I do not use it, and do not advocate it, as it tends to detract from the freedom of the grip.

COMPLETION OF THE BACKHAND DRIVE

Notice the feet are firmly set, with the weight on the right foot, to which it was shifted from the left with the swing. The racquet has struck and passed over the ball, topping it. The body is at right angles to the net, the left arm extended to aid in perfect balance. The whole movement is forward, while the eye is on the ball, in its flight. The stroke in the picture was off a high bounding ball which accounts for the racquet's position being above the wrist in order to bring down the ball. The perfect backhand drive is off the waist, and the racquet passes along that hitting plane. Meet the ball well forward on the backhand, at least in front of the right hip. This will obviate the common error of slicing off to the sideline and will tend to pull the ball into court. The locked wrist, with no turn is essential on all backhand shots below the shoulders. It insures solidity of impact and adds pace to the return. I believe in all beginners playing their backhand shots cross court until they have fully mastered the footwork and locked wrist swing. The common error of slicing the backhand cannot be too strongly emphasised and condemned and cross courting the shot tends to avoid it,

Never allow your opponent to play a shot he likes if you can possibly force him to one he dislikes.

Again I urge that you play your drive:

1. With the body sideways to the net.
2. The swing flat, with long follow through.
3. The weight shifting just as the ball is hit.

Do not strive for terrific speed at first. The most essential thing about a drive is to put the ball in play. I once heard William A. Larned remark, when asked the most important thing in tennis, "Put the ball over the net into the other man's court." Accuracy first, and then put on your speed, for if your shot is correct you can always learn to hit hard.

CHAPTER III

SERVICE

SERVICE is the opening gun of tennis. It is putting the ball in play. The old idea was that service should never be more than merely the beginning of a rally. With the rise of American tennis and the advent of Dwight Davis and Holcombe Ward, service took on a new significance. These two men originated what is now known as the American Twist delivery.

From a mere formality, service became a point winner. Slowly it gained in importance, until Maurice E. M'Loughlin, the wonderful "California Comet," burst across the tennis sky with the first of those terrific cannon-ball deliveries that revolutionized the game, and caused the old-school players to send out hurry calls for a severe footfault rule or some way of stopping the threatened destruction of all ground strokes. M'Loughlin made service a great factor in the game. It remained for R. N. Williams to supply the antidote that has again put service in the normal position of mere importance, not omnipotence. Williams stood in on the delivery and took it on the rising bound.

Service must be speedy. Yet speed is not the be-all and end-all. Service must be accurate, reliable, and varied. It must be used with discretion and served with brains. I believe perfect service is about 40 per cent placement, 40 per cent speed, and 20 per cent twist.

Any tall player has an advantage over a short one, in service. Given a man about 6 feet and allow him the 3 feet added by his reach, it has been proved by tests that should he deliver a service, perfectly flat, with no variation caused by twist or wind, that just cleared the net at its lowest point (3 feet in the centre), there is only a margin of 8 inches of the service court in which the ball can possibly fall; the remainder is below the net angle. Thus it is easy to see how important it is to use some form of twist to bring the ball into court. Not only must it go into court, but it must be sufficiently speedy that the receiver does not have an opportunity of an easy kill. It must also be placed so as to allow the server an advantage for his next return, admitting the receiver puts the ball in play.

Just as the first law of receiving is to put the ball in play, so of service it is to cause the receiver to fall into error. Do not strive unduly for clean aces, but use your service to upset the ground strokes of your opponent.

There are several style services in vogue in all countries. The American twist has become one of the most popular forms of delivery and as such deserves special treatment. The usual forms of service are (1) the slice service, (2) the American twist, (3) the reverse delivery, (4) the "cannon ball" or flat serve.

The slice service is the easiest and most natural form for all beginners, and proves so effective that many great players use it. It is the service of William M. Johnston, A. R. F. Kingscote, Norman E. Brookes, and many others.

Service should be hit from as high a point as the server can *comfortably* reach. To stretch unnecessarily is both wearing on the server and unproductive of results.

The slice service should be hit from a point above the right shoulder and as high as possible. The server should stand at about a forty-five degree angle to the base-line, with both feet firmly planted on the ground. Drop the weight back on the right foot and swing the racquet freely and easily behind the back. Toss the ball high enough into the air to ensure it passing through the desired hitting plane, and then start a slow shift of the weight forward, at the same time increasing the power of the swing forward as the racquet commences its upward flight to the ball. Just as the ball meets the racquet face the weight should be thrown forward and the full power of the swing smashed into the service. Let the ball strike the racquet *inside* the face of the strings, with the racquet travelling directly towards the court. The angle of the racquet face will impart the twist necessary to bring the ball in court. The wrist should be somewhat flexible in service. If necessary lift the right foot and swing the whole body forward with the arm. Twist slightly to the right, using the left foot as a pivot. The general line of the racquet swing is from *right* to *left* and always forward.

At this point and before I take up the other branches of serving, let me put in a warning against footfaulting. I can only say that a footfault is crossing or touching the line with either foot before the ball is delivered, or it is a jump or step. I am not going into a technical discussion of footfaults. It is unnecessary, and by placing your feet firmly before the service there is no need to footfault.

It is just as unfair to deliberately footfault as to miscall a ball, and it is wholly unnecessary. The average footfault is due to carelessness, over-anxiety, or ignorance of the rule. All players are offenders at times, but it can quickly be broken up.

Following this outburst of warning let me return to the American twist service. The stance for this is the same as for the slice, but the ball is thrown slightly to the left of the head while the racquet passes up and over the call, travelling from left to right and slightly forward. The result is a curve to the left and the break of the bound to the right. This service is not fast, but gives an excellent chance to follow to the net, since it travels high and slowly and its bound is deep. The American twist service should be hit with the muscles of the side. The slice is a shoulder swing.

The reverse twist is of an absolutely distinct type. The stance is facing the net with both toes fronting the line. The racquet is gripped as a club. The ball is thrown in front of the body and not high. The swing is a sharp wrist twist from right to left, the ball carried for some distance on the face of the racquet. The curve is from left to right while the bound is high and breaks sharply to the left. This delivery is slow, ineffective and very uncertain. There is little opportunity to follow it to the net.

The "cannon-ball" service is nothing but a slice as regards swing and stance, but it is hit with a flat racquet face, thus imparting no spin to the ball. It is a case of speed alone. This service is a point winner when it goes in; but its average must necessarily be poor since its margin of error is so small. It is only useful to a tall man.

Varied pace and varied speed is the keynote to a good service. I spent hours in serving alone, striving to disguise the twist and pace of the ball. I would take a box of a dozen balls out on the court and serve the whole dozen to No. 1 court with one style of delivery. Then, crossing, I would serve them back with another type of service. Next, I would try the left court from both sides. My next move would be to pick out a certain section of the service court, and serve for that until I could put the ball where I wanted it. Finally, I would strive to put it there with speed.

All the time spent in this practice has stood me in

good stead, for to-day it is my service that pulls me out of many a deep hole, and causes many a player to wish he was delivering the ball. William M. Johnston, the American Champion, has a remarkable service for so short a man. He times his stroke perfectly, and hits it at the top of his reach, so that he gets the full benefit of every inch of his stature and every pound of his weight. He uses the slice delivery in the majority of matches.

Do not try freak services. They are useless against high-class players. Sharp breaking underhand cuts can be easily angled off for points by a man who knows anything of the angles and effects of twist. These deliveries are affectation if used more than once or twice in a long match. A sudden shift may surprise your opponent; but to continue to serve these freaks is to destroy their use.

Mishu, the Rumanian star, has many very peculiar deliveries; but, when playing against high-class tennis, he has brains enough to use a straight service. The freak services delight and yet annoy a gallery, for once the novelty has worn off, nothing but the conceit remains.

The object of service is to obtain the maximum return with the minimum effort. This statement holds true for all tennis strokes, but in none so strongly as in service.

The average player hits his first service so hard, and with so little regard for direction, that about nine out of ten first deliveries are faults. Thus, one half your chances are thrown away, and the chance of double faulting increased proportionately.

There is a well-known tennis saying to the effect that one fault is a mistake, but two faults are a crime—that sums up the idea of service adequately. A player should always strive to put his first delivery in court. In the first place it is apt to catch your opponent napping, as he half expects a fault. Secondly, it conserves your energy by removing the need of a second delivery, which, in a long five-set match, is an item of such importance that it may mean victory or defeat.

I urge all players to put their service into court with just as much speed as they can be sure of, but to serve both deliveries at about the same speed. Do not *slog* the first ball and *pat* the second, but *hit* both with average pace.

Try for service aces whenever reasonable, but never do so at the risk of double faulting. The first ball is the ball to ace. The second should never be risked. Your aces must at least equal your double faults, or your service is a handicap and not an advantage.

The importance of service in doubles is more pronounced than in singles as regards holding it; but the need for individual brilliancy is not so great, as you have a partner already at the net to kill off any weak returns.

Service is an attack, and a successful attack should never break down.

CHAPTER IV

THE VOLLEY AND OVERHEAD SMASH

THE net attack is the heavy artillery of tennis. It is supposed to crush all defence. As such it must be regarded as a point-winning stroke at all times, no matter whether the shot is volley or smash.

Once at the net hit from the point at the first opportunity given to get the racquet squarely on the ball. All the laws of footwork explained for the drive are theoretically the same in volleying. In practice you seldom have time to change your feet to a set position, so you obviate trouble by throwing the weight on the foot nearest to the ball and pushing it in the shot.

Volleys are of two classes: (1) the low volley, made from below the waist; and (2) the high volley, from the waist to the head. In contradistinction to the hitting plane classification are the two styles known as (1) the deep volley and (2) the stop volley.

All low volleys are *blocked*. High volleys may be either *blocked* or *hit*. Volleys should *never be stroked*. There is no follow through on a low volley and very little on a high one.

You will hear much talk of "chop" volleys. A chop stroke is one where the racquet travels from above the line of flight of the ball, down and through it, and the angle made behind the racquet is greater than 45 degrees, and many approach 90 degrees. Therefore I say that no volleys should be chopped, for the tendency is to pop the ball up in the air off any chop. Slice volleys if you want to, or hit them flat, for both these shots are made at a very small angle to the flight-line of the ball, the racquet face travelling almost along its plane.

In all volleys, high or low, the wrist should be locked and absolutely stiff. It should always be below the racquet head, thus bracing the racquet against the impact of the ball. Allow the force of the incoming shot, plus your own weight, to return the ball, and do not strive to "wrist" it over. The tilted racquet face will give any required angle to the return by glancing the ball off the strings, so no wrist turn is needed.

Low volleys can never be hit hard, and owing to the height of the net should usually be sharply angled, to allow distance for the rise. Any ball met at a higher plane than the top of the net may be hit hard. The stroke should be crisp, snappy, and decisive, but it should stop as it meets the ball. The follow through should be very small. Most low volleys should be soft and short. Most high volleys require speed and length.

The "stop" volley is nothing more than a shot blocked short. There is no force used. The rac-

quet simply meets the oncoming ball and stops it.
The ball rebounds and falls of its own weight.
There is little bounce to such a shot, and that may
be reduced by allowing the racquet to slide slightly
under the ball at the moment of impact, thus imparting back spin to the ball.

Volleying is a science based on the old geometric
axiom that a straight line is the shortest distance
between two points. I mean that a volleyer must
always cover the straight passing shot since it is the
shortest shot with which to pass him, and he must
volley straight to his opening and not waste time
trying freakish curving volleys that give the base-
liner time to recover. It is Johnston's great straight
volley that makes him such a dangerous net man.
He is always "punching" his volley straight and
hard to the opening in his opponent's court.

A net player must have ground strokes in order
to attain the net position. Do not think that a
service and volley will suffice against first-class
tennis.

I am not a believer in the "centre" theory.
Briefly expressed the centre theory is to hit down
the middle of the court and follow to the net, since
the other player has the smallest angle to pass you.
That is true, but remember that he has an equal
angle on either side and, given good ground strokes,
an equal chance to pass with only your guess or
intention to tell you which side he will choose.

I advise hitting to the side-line with good length
and following up to the net, coming in just to the

centre side of the straight returns down the line.
Thus the natural shot is covered and your opponent's court is opened for an angle volley 'cross.
Should your opponent try the cross drive, his
chances of beating you clean and keeping the ball
in court are much less than his chances of error.

Strive to kill your volleys at once, but should
your shot not win, follow the ball 'cross and again
cover the straight shot. Always force the man
striving to pass you to play the hardest possible
shot.

Attack with your volleys. Never defend the ball
when at the net. The only defensive volley is one
at your feet as you come in. It is a mid-court shot.
Volleys should win with placement more than speed,
although speed may be used on a high volley.

Closely related to the volley, yet in no way a
volley stroke, is the overhead smash. It is the
Big Bertha of tennis. It is the long range terror
that should always score. The rules of footwork,
position, and direction that govern the volley will
suffice for the overhead. The swing alone is different. The swing should be closely allied to the
slice service, the racquet and arm swinging freely
from the shoulder, the wrist flexible and the racquet
imparting a slight twist to the ball to hold it in
court. The overhead is mainly a point winner
through speed, since its bounce is so high that a
slow placement often allows time for a recovery.

The overhead is about 60 per cent speed, and
40 per cent combined place and twist. Any over-

head shot taken on or within the service-line should be killed. Any overhead behind the service-line, and back to the base-line, should be defended and put back deep to allow you another advance to the net.

The average overhead shot that is missed is netted. Therefore hit deep. It is a peculiar fact that over 75 per cent of all errors are nets with only 25 per cent outs. Let this be a constant reminder to you of the fact that all ground strokes should have a clear margin of safety of some 8 inches to a foot above the net, except when attempting to pass a very active volleyer. In the latter case the shot must be low, and the attendant risk is compensated by the increased chances of winning the point with a pass.

Do not leap in the air unnecessarily to hit overhead balls. Keep at least one foot, and when possible both feet, on the ground in smashing, as it aids in regulating the weight, and gives better balance. Hit flat and decisively to the point if desired.

Most missed overhead shots are due to the eye leaving the ball; but a second class of errors are due to lack of confidence that gives a cramped, half-hearted swing. Follow through your overhead shot to the limit of your swing.

The overhead is essentially a doubles shot, because in singles the chances of passing the net man are greater than lobbing over his head, while in doubles two men cover the net so easily that the best way to open the court is to lob one man back.

In smashing, the longest distance is the safest shot since it allows a greater margin of error. Therefore smash 'cross court when pressed, but pull your short lobs either side as determined by the man you are playing.

Never drop a lob you can hit overhead, as it forces you back and gives the attacking position to your opponent. Never smash with a reverse twist, always hit with a straight racquet face and direct to the opening.

Closely connected to the overhead since it is the usual defence to any hard smash, is the lob.

A lob is a high toss of the ball landing between the service-line and the base-line. An excellent lob should be within 6 feet of the base-line.

Lobs are essentially defensive. The ideas in lobbing are: (1) to give yourself time to recover position when pulled out of court by your opponent's shot; (2) to drive back the net man and break up his attack; (3) to tire your opponent; (4) occasionally to win cleanly by placement. This is usually a lob volley from a close net rally, and is a slightly different stroke.

There is (1) the chop lob, a heavily under-cut spin that hangs in the air. This is the best defensive lob, as it goes high and gives plenty of time to recover position. (2) The stroke lob or flat lob, hit with a slight top spin. This is the point-winning lob since it gives no time to the player to run around

it, as it is lower and faster than the chop. In making this lob, start your swing like a drive, but allow
the racquet to slow up and the face to tilt upward
just as you meet the ball. This shot should seldom
go above 10 feet in the air, since it tends to go out
with the float of the ball.

The chop lob, which is a decided under cut,
should rise from 20 to 30 feet, or more, high and
must go deep. It is better to lob out and run your
opponent back, thus tiring him, than to lob short
and give him confidence by an easy kill. The value
of a lob is mainly one of upsetting your opponent,
and its effects are very apparent if you unexpectedly
bring off one at the crucial period of a match.

I owe one of my most notable victories to a very
timely and somewhat lucky lob. I was playing
Norman E. Brookes in the fifth round of the
American Championships at Forest Hills, in 1919.
The score stood one set all, 3–2 and 30–15,
Brookes serving. In a series of driving returns from
his forehand to my backhand, he suddenly switched
and pounded the ball to my forehand corner and
rushed to the net. I knew Brookes crowded the net,
and with 40–15 or 30-all at stake on my shot, I
took a chance and tossed the ball up in the air over
Brookes' head. It was not a great lob, but it was
a good one. For once Brookes was caught napping,
expecting a drive down the line. He hesitated,
then turned and chased the ball to the back stop,
missing it on his return. I heard him grunt as he
turned, and knew that he was badly winded. He

missed his volley off my return of the next service, and I led at 30–40. The final point of the game came when he again threw me far out of court on my forehand, and, expecting the line drive again, crowded the net, only to have the ball rise in the air over his head. He made a desperate effort at recovery, but failed, and the game was mine: 3-all. It proved the turning-point in the match, for it not only tired Brookes, but it forced him to hang back a little from the net so as to protect his overhead, so that his net attack weakened opportunely, and I was able to nose out the match in 4 sets.

Another famous match won by a lob was the Johnston-Kingscote Davis Cup Match at Wimbledon, in 1920. The score stood 2 sets all, and 5–3 Kingscote leading with Kingscote serving and the score 30-all. Johnston served and ran in. Kingscote drove sharply down Johnston's forehand side-line. Johnston made a remarkable recovery with a half volley, putting the ball high in the air and seemingly outside. A strong wind was blowing down the court and caught the ball and held its flight. It fell on the base-line. Kingscote made a remarkable recovery with a fine lob that forced Johnston back. Kingscote took the net and volleyed decisively to Johnston's backhand. Johnston again lobbed, and by a freak of coincidence the ball fell on the base-line within a foot of his previous shot. Kingscote again lobbed in return, but this time short, and Johnston killed it. Johnston ran out the game in the next two points.

THE FOREHAND VOLLEY

Notice the body at right angles to the net, the left foot advanced to the shot, the weight evenly distributed on the feet, the wrist slightly below the racquet head, the racquet head itself slightly tilted, to lift the volley, and the whole movement a "block" of the ball. The wrist is stiff. There is no swing. The eyes are down, watching the ball. The left arm is the balance wheel. The body crouched and the knees bent.

THE BACKHAND VOLLEY

The body position and weight control and balance are the same as in the forehand volley. The crouch is more pronounced as the hitting plane is lower. The head of the racquet is firmly blocked by the stiff, locked wrist. The eyes are centered on the ball, which has just left the racquet.

If a shot can win two such matches as these, it is a shot worth learning to use, and knowing when to use. The lob is one of the most useful and skilful shots in tennis. It is a great defence and a fine attack.

The strokes already analysed, drive, service, volley, overhead and lob, are the orthodox strokes of tennis, and should be at every player's command. These are the framework of your game. Yet no house is complete with framework alone. There are certain trimmings, ornaments, and decorations necessary. There are the luxuries of modern improvements, and tennis boasts of such improvements in the modern game.

Among the luxuries, some say the eccentricities, of the modern game one finds (1) the chop stroke, (2) the slice stroke (a close relative), (3) the drop shot, (4) the half-volley or "trap" shot.

All these shots have their use. None should be considered a stock shot.

CHAPTER V

CHOP, HALF VOLLEY, AND COURT POSITION

I AM called at times a chop-stroke player. I *seldom chop.* My stroke is a slice.

A chop stroke is a shot where the angle towards the player and behind the racquet, made by the line of flight of the ball, and the racquet travelling down across it, is greater than 45 degrees and may be 90 degrees. The racquet face passes slightly *outside* the ball and down the side, chopping it, as a man chops wood. The spin and curve is from right to left. It is made with a stiff wrist. Irving C. Wright, brother of the famous Beals, is a true chop player, while Beals himself, being a left-hander, chopped from the left court and sliced from the right.

The slice shot merely reduced the angle mentioned from 45 degrees down to a very small one. The racquet face passes either *inside* or *outside* the ball, according to direction desired, while the stroke is mainly a wrist twist or slap. This slap imparts a decided skidding break to the ball, while a chop "drags" the ball off the ground without break. Wallace F. Johnson is the greatest slice exponent in the world.

The rules of footwork for both these shots should be the same as the drive, but because both are made with a short swing and more wrist play, without the need of weight, the rules of footwork may be more safely discarded and body position not so carefully considered.

Both these shots are essentially defensive, and are labour-saving devices when your opponent is on the base-line. A chop or slice is very hard to drive, and will break up any driving game.

It is not a shot to use against a volley, as it is too slow to pass and too high to cause any worry. It should be used to drop short, soft shots at the feet of the net man as he comes in. Do not strive to pass a net man with a chop or slice, except through a big opening.

The drop-shot is a very soft, sharply-angled chop stroke, played wholly with the wrist. It should drop within 3 to 5 feet of the net to be of any use. The racquet face passes around the outside of the ball and under it with a distinct "wrist turn." Do not swing the racquet from the shoulder in making a drop shot. The drop shot has no relation to a stop-volley. The drop shot is all wrist. The stop-volley has no wrist at all.

Use all your wrist shots, chop, slice, and drop, merely as an auxilliary to your orthodox game. They are intended to upset your opponent's game through the varied spin on the ball.

THE HALF VOLLEY

I have now reached the climax of tennis skill: the half volley or trap shot. In other words, the pick-up.

This shot requires more perfect timing, eyesight, and racquet work than any other, since its margin of safety is smallest and its manifold chances of mishaps numberless.

It is a pick-up. The ball meets the ground and racquet face at nearly the same moment, the ball bouncing off the ground, on the strings. This shot is a stiff-wrist, short swing, like a volley with no follow through. The racquet face travels along the ground with a slight tilt over the ball and towards the net, thus holding the ball low; the shot, like all others in tennis, should travel across the racquet face, along the short strings. The racquet face should always be slightly outside the ball.

The half volley is essentially a defensive stroke, since it should only be made as a last resort, when caught out of position by your opponent's shot. It is a desperate attempt to extricate yourself from a dangerous position without retreating. *Never deliberately half volley.*

Notwithstanding these truths, there are certain players who have turned the half volley into a point winner. The greatest half volleyer of the past decade—in fact, one of the greatest tennis geniuses of the world—George Caridia, used the stroke successfully as a point winner. R. N. Williams, the leading exponent of the stroke in the present day, achieves remarkable results with it. Major A. R. F. Kingscote wins many a point, seemingly lost, by his phenomenal half-volley returns, particularly from the base-line. These men turn a defence into an attack, and it pays.

So much for the actual strokes of the game. It is in the other departments such as generalship and psychology that matches are won. Just a few suggestions as to stroke technique, and I will close this section.

Always play your shot with a fixed, definite idea of what you are doing and where it is going. Never hit haphazard.

Play all shots across the short strings of the racquet, with the racquet head and handle on the same hitting plane for ground strokes and the head above the handle for volleys. The racquet head should be advanced slightly beyond the wrist for ground strokes.

COURT POSITION

A tennis court is 39 feet long from base-line to net. Most players think all of that territory is a correct place to stand. Nothing could be farther from the truth. There are only two places in a tennis court that a tennis player should be to await the ball.

1. About 3 feet behind the base-line near the middle of the court, or

2. About 6 to 8 feet back from the net and almost opposite the ball.

The first is the place for all base-line players. The second is the net position.

If you are drawn out of these positions by a shot which you must return, do not remain at the point where you struck the ball, but attain one of the two positions mentioned as rapidly as possible.

The distance from the base-line to about 10 feet from the net may be considered as "no-man's-land" or "the blank." Never linger there, since a deep shot will catch you at your feet. After making your shot from the blank, as you must often do, retreat behind the base-line to await the return, so you may again come forward to meet the ball. If you are drawn in short and cannot retreat safely, continue all the way to the net position.

Never stand and watch your shot, for to do so simply means you are out of position for your next stroke. Strive to attain a position so that you always arrive at the spot the ball is going to before it actually arrives. Do your hard running while the ball is in the air, so you will not be hurried in your stroke after it bounces.

It is in learning to do this that natural anticipation plays a big rôle. Some players instinctively know where the next return is going and take position accordingly, while others will never sense it. It is to the latter class that I urge court position, and recommend always coming in from behind the base-line to meet the ball, since it is much easier to run forward than back.

Should you be caught at the net, with a short shot to your opponent, do not stand still and let him pass you at will, as he can easily do. Pick out the side where you think he will hit, and jump to it suddenly as he swings. If you guess right, you win the point. If you are wrong, you are no worse off, since he would have beaten you anyway with his shot.

A notable example of this method of anticipation is Norman E. Brookes, who instinctively senses the stroke, and suddenly bobs up in front of your best shot and kills it. Some may say it is luck, but, to my mind, it is the reward of brain work.

Your position should always strive to be such that you can cover the greatest possible area of court without sacrificing safety, since the straight shot is the surest, most dangerous, and must be covered. It is merely a question of how much more court than that immediately in front of the ball may be guarded.

A well-grounded knowledge of court position saves many points, to say nothing of much breath expended in long runs after hopeless shots.

It is the phenomenal knowledge of court position that allows A. R. F. Kingscote, a very short man, to attack so consistently from the net. Wallace F. Johnson is seldom caught out of position, so his game is one of extreme ease. One seldom sees

Johnson running hard on a tennis court. He is usually there awaiting the ball's arrival.

Save your steps by using your head. It pays in the end. Time spent in learning where to play on a tennis court is well expended, since it returns to you in the form of matches won, breath saved, and energy conserved.

It is seldom you need cover more than two-thirds of a tennis court, so why worry about the unnecessary portions of it?

PART II: THE LAWS OF TENNIS
PSYCHOLOGY

PART II: THE LAWS OF TENNIS
PSYCHOLOGY

CHAPTER VI

GENERAL TENNIS PSYCHOLOGY

TENNIS psychology is nothing more than understanding the workings of your opponent's mind, and gauging the effect of your own game on his mental viewpoint, and understanding the mental effects resulting from the various external causes on your own mind. You cannot be a successful psychologist of others without first understanding your own mental processes, you must study the effect on yourself of the same happening under different circumstances. You react differently in different moods and under different conditions. You must realize the effect on your game of the resulting irritation, pleasure, confusion, or whatever form your reaction takes. Does it increase your efficiency? If so, strive for it, but never give it to your opponent.

Does it deprive you of concentration? If so, either remove the cause, or if that is not possible strive to ignore it.

Once you have judged accurately your own re-action to conditions, study your opponents', to decide their temperaments. Like temperaments react similarly, and you may judge men of your own type by yourself. Opposite temperaments you must seek to compare with people whose reactions you know.

A person who can control his own mental pro-cesses stands an excellent chance of reading those of another, for the human mind works along definite lines of thought, and can be studied. One can only control one's mental processes after carefully studying them.

A steady phlegmatic base-line player is seldom a keen thinker. If he was he would not adhere to the base-line.

The physical appearance of a man is usually a pretty clear index to his type of mind. The stolid, easy-going man, who usually advocates the base-line game, does so because he hates to stir up his torpid mind to think out a safe method of reaching the net. There is the other type of base-line player, who prefers to remain on the back of the court while directing an attack intended to break up your game. He is a very dangerous player, and a deep, keen-thinking antagonist. He achieves his results by mixing up his length and direction, and worrying you with the variety of his game. He is a good psychologist. Such players include J. C. Parke, Wallace F. Johnson, and Charles S. Garland. The first type of player mentioned merely hits the ball with little idea of what he is doing, while the latter always has a definite plan and adheres to it. The hard-hitting, erratic, net-rushing player is a creature of impulse. There is no real system to his attack, no understanding of your game. He will make brilliant *coups* on the spur of the moment, largely by instinct; but there is no mental power of consistent thinking. It is an interesting, fascinating type. Such men as Harold Throckmorton, B. I. C. Norton, and at times R. N. Williams, are examples, although Williams is really a better psychologist than this sounds.

The dangerous man is the player who mixes his style from back to fore court at the direction of an ever-alert mind. This is the man to study and learn from. He is a player with a definite purpose. A player who has an answer to every query you propound him in your game. He is the most subtle antagonist in the world. He is of the school of Brookes. Second only to him is the man of dogged determination that sets his mind on one plan and adheres to it, bitterly, fiercely fighting to the end, with never a thought of change. He is the man whose psychology is easy to understand, but whose mental viewpoint is hard to upset, for he never allows himself to think of anything except the business at hand. This man is your Johnston or your Wilding. I respect the mental capacity of Brookes more, but I admire the tenacity of purpose of Johnston.

Pick out your type from your own mental processes, and then work out your game along the lines best suited to you. Few of us have the mental brilliance of Brookes; but all can acquire the dogged determination of Johnston, even if we have not his tennis ability.

When two men are in the same class as regards stroke equipment, the determining factor in any given match is the mental viewpoint. Luck, so-called, is often grasping the psychological value of a break in the game, and turning it to your own account.

We hear a great deal about the "shots we have made." Few realize the importance of the "shots we have missed." The science of missing shots is as important as that of making them, and at times a miss by an inch is of more value than a return that is killed by your opponent.

Let me explain. A player drives you far out of court with an angle shot. You run hard to it, and reaching, drive it hard and fast down the side-line, missing it by an inch. Your opponent is surprised and shaken, realizing that your shot might as well have gone in as out. He will expect you to try it again, and will not take the risk next time. He will try to play the ball, and may fall into error. You have thus taken some of your opponent's confidence, and increased his chance of error, all by a miss.

If you had merely popped back that return, and it had been killed, your opponent would have felt increasingly confident of your inability to get the ball out of his reach, while you would merely have been winded without result.

Let us suppose you made the shot down the sideline. It was a seemingly impossible get. First it amounts to *two* points in that it took one away from your opponent that should have been his and gave you one you ought never to have had. It also worries your opponent, as he feels he has thrown away a big chance.

The psychology of a tennis match is very interesting, but easily understandable. Both men start with equal chances. Once one man establishes a real lead, his confidence goes up, while his opponent worries, and his mental viewpoint becomes poor. The sole object of the first man is to hold his lead, thus holding his confidence. If the second player pulls even or draws ahead, the inevitable reaction occurs with even a greater contrast in psychology. There is the natural confidence of the leader now with the second man as well as that great stimulus of having turned seeming defeat into probable victory. The reverse in the case of the first player is apt to hopelessly destroy his game, and collapse follows.

It is this twist in tennis psychology that makes it possible to win so many matches after they are seemingly lost. This is also the reason that a man who has lost a substantial lead seldom turns in the ultimate victory. He cannot rise above the depression caused by his temporary slump. The value of an early lead cannot be overestimated. It is the ability to control your mental processes, and not worry unduly over early reverses, that makes a great match player.

Playing to the score is the first requisite of a thinking match player. The two crucial points in any game are the third and fourth. If the first two points are divided for 15-all, the third means an advantage gained. If won by you, you should strive to consolidate it by taking the next for 40–15 and two chances for game, while if lost, you must draw even at 30-all to have an even chance for game.

In order to do this, be sure to always put the ball in play safely, and do not take unnecessary chances, at 15-all or 30–15. Always make the server work to hold his delivery. It worries him to serve long games, and increases the nervous strain of the match.

In the game score the sixth, seventh, and eighth games are the crux of every close set. These games may mean 4–2 or 3-all, 5–2 or 4–3, the most vital advantage in the match, or 5–3 or 4-all, a matter of extreme moment to a tiring player. If ahead, you should strive to hold and increase your lead. If behind, your one hope of victory rests in cutting down the advantage of the other man *before* one slip means defeat. 5–2 is usually too late to start a rally, but 4–3 is a real chance.

Never throw away a set because a player has a lead of 4–1, or even 5–1, unless you already have two sets in a 5-set match, and do not wish to risk

DAVIS CUP CHALLENGE ROUND, 1921
Zenzo Shimidzu, *Japan* and William T. Tilden 2nd, *America*, just previous to the opening of their terrific match in which Shimidzu led by two sets, 5-4 and 30-0, only to have the American finally pull out the victory.

DAVIS CUP CHALLENGE ROUND, 1921

William M. Johnston, *America* and Ichiya Kumagae, *Japan*, take the court for the opening match before a gallery of over 12,000 people. Johnston won in sequence sets, scoring the first point for America.

tiring by trying to pull it out, and possibily failing
at 6–4. The great advantage of 3–1 on your own
service is a stumbling-block for many players, for
they unconsciously let up at the fifth game, thinking
they have a 2-game lead. However, by dropping
that game, the score will go 2–3 and 3-all if your
opponent holds service, instead of 1–4 and 4–2,
thus retaining a distinct advantage and discouraging
your opponent in that set.

The first set is vital in a 2 out of 3 match. Play
for all of it. The second and third sets are the
turning-point in a best of 5-set match. Take the
first where possible, but play to the limit for the
next two. Never allow a 3 out of 5-set match to
go to the fifth set if it is possible to win in less;
but never give up a match until the last point is
played, even if you are two sets and five games down.
Some occurrence may turn the tide in your favour.

A notable example of such a match occurred at
Newport, in 1916. Wallace F. Johnson and
Joseph J. Armstrong were playing Ichija Kumagae,
the famous Japanese star, and Harold A. Throckmorton, then Junior Champion of America, in the
second round of the doubles.

It was Kumagae's first year in America, and he
did not understand Americans and their customs
well. Kumagae and Throckmorton were leading
one set at 6–0, 5–1, and 40–15, Kumagae serving.
Throckmorton turned and spoke to him, and the
Japanese star did not understand what he said.
He served without knowing, and Armstrong passed

him down the centre. Johnson duplicated the feat in the next court, and Kumagae grew flustered. Throckmorton, not understanding, tried to steady him without result, as Kumagae double-faulted to Armstrong, and he, too, grew worried. Both men began missing, and Johnson and Armstrong pulled out the set and won the match in a runaway in the last stanza. Johnson and Armstrong met W. M. Johnston and C. J. Griffin, the National Champions, in the final and defeated them in five sets, inflicting the only reverse the title-holders suffered during their two-year reign as champions.

Another much more regrettable incident occurred in the famous match between R. L. Murray of California and George M. Church of New York in the fourth round of the American National Championship in 1916. George Church, then at the crest of his wonderful game, had won the first two sets and was leading Murray in the third, when the famous Californian started a sensational rally. Murray, with his terrific speed, merry smile, and genial personality, has always been a popular figure with the public, and when he began his seemingly hopeless fight, the crowd cheered him wildly. He broke through Church's service and drew even amid a terrific din. Church, always a very high-strung, nervous player, showed that the crowd's partiality was getting on his nerves. The gallery noticed it, and became more partisan than ever. The spirit of mob rule took hold, and for once they lost all sense of sportsmanship. They clapped errors as they rained from Church's racquet; the great game collapsed under the terrific strain, and Church's last chance was gone. Murray won largely as he wanted, in the last two sets. No one regretted the incident more than Murray himself, for no finer sportsman steps upon the court than this player, yet there was nothing that could be done. It was a case of external conditions influencing the psychology of one man so greatly that it cost him a victory that was his in justice.

The primary object in match tennis is to break up the other man's game. The first lesson to learn is to hold your nerve under all circumstances. If you can break a player's nerve by pounding at a weakness, do it. I remember winning a 5-set doubles match many years ago, against a team far over the class of my partner and myself, by lobbing continually to one man until he cracked under the strain and threw the match away. He became so afraid of a lob that he would not approach the net, and his whole game broke up on account of his lack of confidence. Our psychology was good, for we had the confidence to continue our plan of attack even while losing two of the first three sets. His was bad, for he lost his nerve, and let us know it.

Sensational and unexpected shots at crucial moments have won many a match. If your opponent makes a marvellous recovery and wins by it, give him full credit for it, and then forget it, for by worrying over it you not only lose that point but several others as well, while your mind is still wan-

dering.   Never lose your temper over your opponent's good shots.   It is bad enough to lose it at
your own bad ones.   Remember that usually the
loser of a match plays just as well as the winner
allows him.   Never lose your temper at a bad decision.   It never pays, and has cost many a match.

I remember a famous match in Philadelphia, between Wallace F. Johnson, the fifth ranking player
in America, and Stanley W. Pearson, a local star,
in the Interclub tennis league of that city.   Johnson,
who had enjoyed a commanding lead of a set and
4–1, had slumped, and Pearson had pulled even at
a set-all, and was leading at 5–1 and 40–15, point
set match.   He pulled Johnson far out to the forehand and came to the net.   Johnson chopped
viciously down the side-line, but Pearson volleyed
to Johnson's deep backhand corner.   Johnson had
started *running* in that direction as he hit his return,
and arrived almost as Pearson's volley bounced.
Unfortunately Johnson slipped and went down on
both knees, but held his racquet.   He reached the
ball and chopped it down the side-line for an earned
point before Pearson realized he had even offered
at it.

Pearson was so surprised and angered that he
double-faulted for deuce, and Johnson won the
game.   Johnson pulled even at 5-all, before Pearson
recovered his equilibrium, and finally won the set
at 17–15.   Truly Pearson's lapse at Johnson's marvellous get was a costly mental break.

Tennis psychology is far more than the effect of

certain shots, made or missed, on the player. One can sum up such things by saying that every kill gives confidence, every error tends to destroy it. These things are obvious. The branch of psychology that is interesting is the reaction on the various players of different courts, different crowds, and other players.

There is a peculiar atmosphere about the centre court at Wimbledon that is unique in my knowledge of the game. Certain players revel in it. The majority do not feel it, and since they do not sense it, they find only the material disadvantages of rather bad light, and much noise from the stand, and dislike the centre court. Personally, I enjoy playing on the centre court at Wimbledon more than any court I have ever stepped upon.

The traditions of the great players of the past, the notable personages that make up the parties in the Royal Box and Committee Box, the honour of a visit from their Majesties the King and Queen, and, above all, the generous, non-partisan, sportsmanlike attitude of the British public, make it a unique privilege to enter the centre court in championship competition. These things inspire the mind to an almost abnormal keenness. It is this atmosphere that made N. E. Brookes, Anthony F. Wilding, A. W. Gore, R. F. and H. L. Doherty more dangerous there than anywhere else. It is this factor that spurs on J. C. Parke and A. R. F. Kingscote to their greatest tennis to-day.

The great championship turf at Forest Hills,

where the American Championship is held, offers a unique contrast to Wimbledon.

The age of Wimbledon is its great attraction. It is the spirit of youth, of progress, of business-like mechanical perfection of management, and the enormous crowds and attendant enthusiasm that is the chief attraction at Forest Hills. Fully 15,000 were present on the closing day of the event in 1919. Orderly, courteous, enthusiastic, but partisan, the American tennis public comes out to cheer on its favourite. No people in the world appreciate visiting players more whole-heartedly and none do more for their comfort than the American people. It is partisan, personal, sporting friendliness, warmer yet not so correct as the manner of the British public, that the Americans give. We have much to learn from our British friends. Yet I hope we will never sacrifice the warmth of feeling that at times may run away with us, yet in the main is the chief attraction of the American people. It is this enthusiasm that spurs on the men to their greatest efforts in the National Championship.

The Australian team, Norman E. Brookes, Gerald Patterson, Randolph Lycett, and R. V. Thomas, who visited the United States in 1919, scored a unique personal triumph. The whole gallery present at the notable match in the Championship, when Patterson went down to defeat in a terrific 5-set struggle with W. M. Johnston, rose and cheered Patterson as he walked off the court. It was a real ovation; a tribute to his sportsmanship, and an outburst of personal admiration. Brookes was the recipient of an equal demonstration on his final appearance at Forest Hills. The stimulus of the surroundings produced the highest tennis of which these men were capable.

Yet in all championships it is the personal element that is ,the moving factor. Personalities are the deciding force in popularity. Patriotism is partially submerged in personality.

The Davis Cup matches bring out the gamest struggles in the history of tennis. It is in these unique series of matches that the fame of Anthony F. Wilding, Norman E. Brookes, J. C. Parke, B. C. Wright, M. E. M'Loughlin, and others reached its crest. It was the unselfish giving of one's best, under all conditions, for the honour of the country that called out the finest tennis in each man. Parke reached his crest in his memorable defeat of Brookes. M'Loughlin has never quite equalled his marvellous game of 1914 against Brookes and Wilding.

It is the psychology of patriotism that brings out this tennis.

Personality is submerged. Unity of purpose as a team, replaces the object of personal glory that is the keynote of championship.

It is the friendly rivalry of sport, between such men as form the backbone of tennis in each country, that does more for international understanding than all the notes ever written from the White House.

I could go on writing tennis psychology as explained by external conditions for hundreds of pages, but all I want to do is to bring to mind a definite idea of the value of the mind in the game. Stimulate it how you will, a successful tennis player must admit the value of quick mind. Do it by a desire for personal glory, or team success, or by a love of competition in matching your wits against the other man's, but do it some way.

Do. not think that tennis is merely a physical exercise. It is a mental cock-tail of a very high "kick."

CHAPTER VII

THE PSYCHOLOGY OF MATCH PLAY,

THE first and most important point in match play is to know how to lose. Lose cheerfully, generously, and like a sportsman. This is the first great law of tennis, and the second is like unto it—to win modestly, cheerfully, generously, and like a sportsman.

The object of match play is to win, but no credit goes to a man who does not win fairly and squarely. A victory is a defeat if it is other than fair. Yet again I say to win is the object, and to do so, one should play to the last ounce of his strength, the last gasp of his breath, and the last scrap of his nerve. If you do so and lose, the better man won. If you do not, you have robbed your opponent of his right of beating your best. Be fair to both him and yourself.

"The Play's the thing," and in match play a good defeat is far more creditable than a hollow victory. Play tennis for the game's sake. Play it for the men you meet, the friends you make, and the pleasure you may give to the public by the hard-working yet sporting game that is owed them by their presence at the match.

Many tennis players feel they owe the public

nothing, and are granting a favour by playing. It is my belief that when the public so honours a player that they attend matches, that player is in duty bound to give of his best, freely, willingly, and cheerfully, for only by so doing can he repay the honour paid him. The tennis star of to-day owes his public as much as the actor owes the audience, and only by meeting his obligations can tennis be retained in public favour. The players get their reward in the personal popularity they gain by their conscientious work.

There is another factor that is even stronger than this, that will always produce fine tennis in championship events. It is the competitive spirit that is the breath of life to every true sportsman: the desire to prove to himself he can beat the best of the other man; the real regret that comes when he wins, and feels the loser was not at his best. It is that which has made popular idols of Anthony F. Wilding, M. E. M'Loughlin, and other famous players. It is the great attraction of J. C. Parke, A. R. F. Kingscote, W. M. Johnston, André Gobert, W. Laurentz, and many other stars. It is the sign of a true sportsman.

The keen competitive spirit that stimulates a match player also increases the nervous strain. This should be recognized by tournament committees, and the conditions of play should be as nearly standardized as weather permits.

A tournament committee should never keep a player waiting for an important match to commence while they scour through the crowd for linesmen. These necessary, and I trust useful, accessories to every match of importance should be picked and on hand when the players appear. A good linesman is a great aid to match tennis. A poor one may ruin a great battle. Not only will bad decisions turn the tide by putting a point in the wrong columns, but slow decisions will often upset players, so they dare not play to the line kept by slumberous linesmen.

A linesman should take his first judgment as the ball strikes. If outside he should call "out" at once clearly, decisively, but not too loudly; a yell is often a shock to the nerves. If the ball is good he should remain discreetly silent.

The umpire should announce the score after each point in a voice sufficiently loud to be heard by the entire gallery. His decisions as to "lets" or balls "not up" should be made only loud enough to ensure that they are heard by the players. The gallery has eyes. Following each game, the game score should be called, giving the leading player's name and the set being played. For example, "Four games to three, Parke leads. Second set." About every third game following the completion of the first set, an announcement as to the winner of the first set is an excellent idea. The umpire could add to the above announcement, "First set, Parke, 6-3." This latter announcement is unnecessary when there is a score board that gives full details of the match.

Tournament committees should see that all courts have sufficient room behind the base-line and at the sides to insure a player against running into the stops.

Galleries should strive to retain their appreciation and enthusiasm until a point is completed, since noise is very disconcerting to a player. However, all players enjoy an enthusiastic gallery.

The players themselves must now be considered in relation to the reaction of the match.

The first thing to fix firmly in your mind in playing a match, is never to allow your opponent to play a shot he likes if it is possible to force him to make one he does not. Study your opponent both on and off the court. Look for a weakness, and, once finding it, pound it without mercy. Remember that you do not decide your mode of attack. It is decided for you by the weakness of your opponent. If he dislikes to meet a netman, go to the net. If he wants you at the net, stay back and force him to come in. If he attacks viciously, meet his attack with an equally strong offensive.

Remember that the strongest defence is to attack, for if the other man is occupied in meeting your attack, he will have less time to formulate his own system.

If you are playing a very steady man, do not strive to beat him at his own game. He is better at it than you in many cases, so go in and hit to win. On the other hand, if you find that your opponent is wild and prone to miss, play safe and reap the full crop of his errors. It saves you trouble and takes his confidence.

Above all, never change a winning game.

Always change a losing game, since, as you are getting beaten that way, you are no worse off and may be better with a new style.

The question of changing a losing game is a very serious thing. It is hard to say just when you are really beaten. If you feel you are playing well yet have lost the first set about 6–3 or 6–4, with the loss of only one service, you should not change. Your game is not really a losing game. It is simply a case of one break of service, and might well win the next set. If, however, you have dropped the first set in a 2 out of 3 match with but one or two games, now you are outclassed and should try something else.

Take chances when you are behind, never when ahead. Risks are only worth while when you have everything to win and nothing to lose. It may spell victory, and at least will not hasten defeat. Above all, never lose your nerve or confidence in a match. By so doing you have handed your opponent about two points a game—a rather hard handicap to beat at your best.

Never let your opponent know you are worried. Never show fatigue or pain if it is possible to avoid, since it will only give him confidence. Remember that he feels just as bad as you, and any sign of weakening on your part encourages him to go on.

In other words, keep your teeth always in the match.

Don't worry. Don't fuss. Luck evens up in the long run, and to worry only upsets your own game without affecting your opponent. A smile wins a lot of points because it gives the impression of confidence on your part that shakes that of the other man. Fight all the time. The harder the strain the harder you should fight, but do it easily, happily, and enjoy it.

Match play, where both men are in the same class as tennis players, resolves itself into a battle of wits and nerve. The man who uses the first and retains the second is the ultimate victor.

I do not believe in a man who expects to go through a long tournament, going "all out" for every match. Conserve your strength and your finesse for the times you need them, and win your other matches decisively, but not destructively. Why should a great star discourage and dishearten a player several classes below him by crushing him, as he no doubt could? A few games a set, well earned, would be a big factor in encouraging that rising player to play in tournaments, while it would in no way injure the reputation of the star.

Never hurry your opponent by serving before he is fully set to receive. This is a favourite trick of a few unscrupulous players, yet is really an unfair advantage. Do your hurrying after the ball is in play, by running him to unexpected places in the court. Should anyone attempt to work the hurried service on you, after several attempts, proving it is intentional, let the ball go by and say "not ready." The server will shortly realize that you will take your time regardless of him, and he will slow up.

I do not advocate stalling—nothing is worse. It is a breach of ethics that is wholly uncalled for. Play the game naturally, and give your opponent full courtesy in all matters. If you do, you will receive it in return.

Take every advantage of any and every weakness in your opponent's game; but never trespass on his rights as regards external advantages.

Personally I do not believe in "defaulting" a match. To "scratch" or "retire," as the term goes, is to cheat your opponent of his just triumph, and you should never do this unless it is absolutely impossible to avoid. Sickness or some equally important reason should be the sole cause of scratching, for you owe the tournament your presence once your entry is in.

Match play should stimulate a player. He should produce his best under the excitement of competition. Learn your shots in practice, but use them in matches.

Practice is played with the racquet, matches are won by the mind. J. C. Parke is a great match player, because he is not only a great player but a great student of men. He sizes up his opponent, and seizes every opening and turns it to his own account. Norman E. Brookes is the greatest match player the world has ever known, because he is ever ready to change his plan to meet the strategy of his opponent, and has both the variety of stroke and versatility of intellect to outguess the other the majority of times. Brookes is the greatest court general, and, in my opinion, the finest tennis intellect in the world. His mind is never so keen and he is never so dangerous as when he is trailing in an important match. He typifies all that is great in mental match tennis.

A great star is always at his best in a match, as it stimulates his mental and physical faculties to the utmost.

Certain players are more effective against some men than others who are not so good. It is the uncertainty of match tennis that is its greatest charm. Two men may meet for tennis during a season, and be so closely matched that each man will win two matches and the score seem almost one-sided each time. It is a case of getting the jump on the other player.

During 1919 Johnston and I met four times. Twice he defeated me, once in four sets, and once in three, while the two victories that were mine were scored in identically the same number of sets. The most remarkable meeting of two stars was the series of matches between R. L. Murray and Ichija Kumagae during the seasons of 1918 and 1919. In the early stages Murray had a decided advantage, winning from Kumagae consistently, but by close scores. Early in 1919 Kumagae unexpectedly defeated Murray at Buffalo in four sets. From that

NORMAN E. BROOKES AND GERALD L. PATTERSON
Australia, 1920

R. M. WILLIAMS, 2ND AND
WATSON M. WASHBURN
America, 1921

M. E. MC LOUGHLIN AND
T. C. BUNDY
America, 1914

FAMOUS DAVIS CUP DOUBLES TEAMS

NORMAN E. BROOKES.
Australia

ANTHONY F. WILDING
New Zealand

BEALS WRIGHT
America

W. A. LARNED
America

FAMOUS DAVIS CUP STARS

moment Kumagae held the whip hand. He defeated Murray at Niagara-on-the-Lake a week later. Murray barely nosed out the Japanese star at Cleveland in five sets after Kumagae had the match won, only to have Kumagae again defeat him in a terrific match at Newport in August.

Kumagae's game is very effective against Murray, because Murray, essentially a volleyer, could not exchange ground strokes with the Japanese star player successfully, and could not stand the terrific pace of rushing the net at every opportunity. Kumagae conclusively proved his slight superiority over Murray last season.

Vincent Richards, who is not yet the equal of Murray, scored two clean-cut victories over Kumagae during the same period. Why should Richards worry Kumagae, who is certainly Murray's superior, and yet not cause Murray trouble?

The answer lies in this style of game. Richards uses a peculiar chop stroke from the base-line that is very steady. He can meet Kumagae at his own base-line game until he gets a chance to close in to the net, where his volleying is remarkable. The result is, against Kumagae's driving he is perfectly at home. Murray is a vicious net player who swept Richards off his feet. The boy has not the speed on his ground strokes to pass Murray, who volleys off his chop for points, and cannot take the net away from him as he cannot handle the terrific speed of Murray's game. Thus Murray's speed beats Richards, while Richards' steadiness troubles

Kumagae, yet Kumagae's persistent driving tires Murray and beats him. What good are comparative scores?

Charles S. Garland always defeats Howard Voshell, yet loses to men whom Voshell defeats. Williams proves a stumbling-block to Johnston, yet seldom does well against me.

The moral to be drawn from the ever-interesting upsets that occur every year, is that the style of your attack should be determined by the man's weakness you are playing. Suit your style to his weakness. A chop is the antidote for the drive. The volley is the answer to a chop, yet a drive is the only safe attack against a volley. The smash will kill a lob, yet a lob is the surest defence from a smash. Rather a complicated condition, but one which it would do well to think over.

The most dangerous enemy to R. N. Williams is a steady base-liner of second class. Williams is apt to crush a top-flight player in a burst of superlative terms, yet fall a victim to the erratic streak that is in him when some second-class player plays pat-ball with him. Such defeats were his portion at the hands of Ritchie and Mavrogordato in England, yet on the same trip he scored notable victories over Parke and Johnston.

Abnormal conditions for match play always tend to affect the better player more than the poorer, and bring play to a level.

The reason for this is in the fact that the higher the standard of a player's game, the smaller his margin of error, the more perfect his bound must be, and any variation from the normal is apt to spell error. The average player allows himself more leeway, and unknowingly increases his chances on a bad court. His shot is not judged to the fraction of an inch in swing as is the top-flight player, so a slight variation does not affect him.

Many a great match has been ruined by abnormal conditions. Rain caused Williams' downfall to N. W. Niles in the 1917 American Championships. Rain and wind marred a great battle between Gobert and Johnston at Eastbourne in the Davis Cup in 1920.

The clever match player must always be willing to change his game to meet conditions. Failure to do so may spell defeat.

It is this uncertainty, due to external conditions, that makes comparative records so useless in judging the relative merits of two players you know nothing of. Rankings based on mathematical calculations of scores are absolutely useless and childish, unless tempered by common sense.

The question of the fitness of conditions of play can never be standardized. In America you play only if clear. In England sometimes when clear but more often in rain, judging by the events I swam through in my recent trip. A match player should not only be able to play tennis, but should combine the virtues of an aeroplane and a submarine as well.

CHAPTER VIII

THE PSYCHOLOGY OF PHYSICAL FITNESS

PHYSICAL fitness is one of the great essentials of match play. Keenness can only be acquired if the physical, mental, and nervous systems are in tune. Consistent and systematic training is essential to a tournament player.

Regular hours of sleep, and regular, hearty food at regular hours are necessary to keep the body at its highest efficiency. Food is particularly important. Eat well, but do not over-eat, particularly immediately before playing. I believe in a large hearty breakfast on the day of a big match. This should be taken by nine-thirty. A moderate lunch at about one o'clock if playing at three. Do not eat very rich food at luncheon as it tends to slow you up on the court. Do not run the risk of indigestion, which is the worst enemy to clear eyesight. Rich, heavy food immediately before retiring is bad, as it is apt to make you "loggy" on the court the next day.

It is certain injury to touch alcoholic drink in any form during tournament play. Alcohol is a poison that affects the eye, the mind, and the wind—three essentials in tennis. Tobacco in moderation does little harm, although it, too, hits eye and wind. A man who is facing a long season of tournament play should refrain from either alcohol or tobacco in any form. Excesses of any kind are bad for physical condition, and should not be chanced.

Late hours cause sluggishness of mind and body the next day. It is very dangerous to risk them before a hard match. The moving pictures immediately before playing tennis are bad, owing to the eye strain caused by the flicker of the film and the strong light of the camera. Lead a normal, healthy life, and conserve your nervous force wherever possible, as you will need it in the hard matches.

"Staleness" is the great enemy of players who play long seasons. It is a case of too much tennis. Staleness is seldom physical weariness. A player can always recover his strength by rest. Staleness is a mental fatigue due often to worry or too close attention to tennis, and not enough variety of thought. Its symptoms are a dislike for the tennis game and its surroundings, and a lack of interest in the match when you are on the court. I advocate a break in training at such a time. Go to the theatre or a concert, and get your mind completely off tennis. Do your worrying about tennis while you are playing it, and forget the unpleasantness of bad play once you are off the court. Always have some outside interest you can turn to for relaxation during a tournament; but never allow it to interfere with your tennis when you should be intent on your game. A nice balance is hard to achieve, but once

attained is a great aid to a tournament player. I
find my relaxation in auction bridge. I know many
other players who do likewise. Among them are
Mrs. Franklin Mallory, Wallace F. Johnson, W.
M. Johnston and Samuel Hardy.

The laws of training should be closely followed
before and after a match. Do not get chilled before
a match, as it makes you stiff and slow. Above all
else do not stand around without a wrap after a
match when you are hot or you will catch cold.

Many a player has acquired a touch of rheuma-
tism from wasting time at the close of his match instead of getting his shower while still warm. That
slight stiffness the next day may mean defeat. A
serious chill may mean severe illness. Do not take
chances.

Change your wet clothes to dry ones between
matches if you are to play twice in a day. It will
make you feel better, and also avoid the risk of
cold.

Tournament players must sacrifice some pleasures
for the sake of success. Training will win many a
match for a man if he sticks to it. Spasmodic
training is useless, and should never be attempted.

The condition a player is in is apt to decide his
mental viewpoint, and aid him in accustoming himself to the external conditions of play.

All match players should know a little about the
phenomenon of crowd-psychology since, as in the
case of the Church-Murray match I related some

time back, the crowd may play an important part
in the result.

It seldom pays to get a crowd down on you. It
always pays to win its sympathy. I do not mean
play to the gallery, for that will have the opposite
effect than the one desired.

The gallery is always for the weaker player. It
is a case of helping the "under-dog." If you are
a consistent winner you must accustom yourself to
having the gallery show partiality for your opponent. It is no personal dislike of you. It is merely
a natural reaction in favour of the loser. Sometimes a bad decision to one play will win the crowd's
sympathy for him. Galleries are eminently just in
their desires, even though at times their emotions
run away with them.

Quite aside from the effect on the gallery, I wish
to state here that when you are the favoured one
in a decision that you know is wrong, strive to equal-
ize it if possible by unostentatiously losing the next
point. Do not hit the ball over the back stop or
into the bottom of the net with a jaunty air of
"Here you are." Just hit it slightly out or in the
net, and go on about your business in the regular
way. Your opponent always knows when you ex-
tend him this justice, and he appreciates it, even
though he does not expect it. Never do it for effect.
It is extremely bad taste. Only do it when your
sense of justice tells you you should.

The crowd objects, and justly so, to a display of
real temper on the court. A player who loses his

head must expect a poor reception from the gallery. Questioned decisions by a player only put him in a bad light with the crowd and cannot alter the point. You may know the call was wrong, but grin at it, and the crowd will join you. These things are the essence of good sportsmanship, and good sportsmanship will win any gallery. The most unattractive player in the world will win the respect and admiration of a crowd by a display of real sportsmanship at the time of test.

Any player who really enjoys a match for the game's sake will always be a fine sportsman, for there is no amusement to a match that does not give your opponent his every right. A player who plays for the joy of the game wins the crowd the first time he steps on the court. All the world loves an optimist.

The more tennis I play, the more I appreciate my sense of humour. I seldom play a match when I do not get a smile out of some remark from the gallery, while I know that the gallery always enjoys at least one hearty laugh at my expense. I do not begrudge it them, for I know how very peculiar tennis players in general, and myself in particular, appear when struggling vainly to reach a shot hopelessly out of reach.

Two delightful elderly ladies were witnessing Charles S. Garland and myself struggle against Mavrogordato and Riseley at the Edgbaston tournament in England in 1920. One turned to the other and said: "Those are the Americans!"

THE 1921 AUSTRALIAN DAVIS CUP TEAM
J. O. Anderson, J. B. Hawkes, Norman Peach and C. V. Todd.

THE 1920 AMERICAN DAVIS CUP TEAM
R. N. Williams, 2nd, W. M. Johnston, Captain Samuel Hardy, W. T. Tilden, 2nd
and C. S. Garland.

"Oh," said the second lady resignedly, "I thought so. The tall one [meaning me] looks rather queer."

During the Davis Cup match against the French at Eastbourne, I went on the court against Laurentz in my blue "woolly" sweater. The day was cold, and I played the match 4–1 in Laurentz' favour, still wearing it. I started to remove it at the beginning of the sixth game, when the gallery burst into loud applause, out of which floated a sweet feminine voice: "Good! Now maybe the poor boy will be able to play!"

For the first time I realized just what the gallery thought of my efforts to play tennis, and also of the handicap of the famous "blue-bearskin" as they termed it.

My favourite expression during my Davis Cup trip happened to be "Peach" for any particularly good shot by my opponent. The gallery at the Championship, quick to appreciate any mannerism of a player, and to know him by it, enjoyed the remark on many occasions as the ball went floating by me. In my match with Kingscote in the final set, the court was very slippery owing to the heavy drizzle that had been falling throughout the match. At 3–2 in my favour, I essayed a journey to the net, only to have Kingscote pass me 'cross court to my backhand. I turned and started rapidly for the shot murmuring "Peach" as I went. Suddenly my feet went out and I rolled over on the ground, sliding some distance, mainly on my face. I arose,

dripping, just in time to hear, *sotto voce,* in the gallery at my side: "A little bit crushed, that Peach."
The sense of humour of the speaker was delightful.
The whole side-line howled with joy, and the joke
was on me.

I am always the goat for the gallery in these
little jokes, because it is seldom I can refrain from
saying something loud enough to be heard.

I remember an incident that caused great joy to
a large gallery in Philadelphia during a match between two prominent local players. One of the men
had been charging the net and volleying consistently
off the frame of his racquet, giving a wonderful display of that remarkable shot known the world over
as "the mahogany volley." His luck was phenomenal for all his mis-hit volleys won him points. Finally, at the end of a bitterly contested deuce game
in the last set he again won the deciding point with
a volley off the wood, just as a small insect flew in
his eye.

He called to his opponent: "Just a moment, I
have a fly in my eye."

The disgusted opponent looked up and muttered:
"Fly? Huh! I'll bet it's a splinter!"

There was a certain young player who was notori-
ously lax in his eyesight on decisions. He could
never see one against himself. He became noted
in his own locality. He and another boy were
playing a team of brothers who were quite famous
in the tennis world. One of these brothers had a
very severe service that the local Captain Kidd could

not handle at all. So each time the visiting player served close to the line, the boy would swing at it, miss it, and call "Fault!" There was no umpire available and there was no question of the older team losing, so they let it go for some time. Finally a service fully 3 feet in was casually called out by the youngster. This proved too much for the server, who hailed his brother at the net with the query: "What was wrong that time?"

"I don't know," came the reply; "unless he called a footfault on you!"

The assurance of some young players is remarkable. They know far more about the game of other men than the men themselves. I once travelled to a tournament with a boy who casually seated himself beside me in the train and, seeing my tennis bag, opened the conversation on tennis and tennis players. He finally turned his attention to various people I knew well, and suddenly burst out with: "Tilden is a chop-stroke player. I know him well." I let him talk for about ten minutes, learning things about my game that I never knew before. Finally I asked his name, which he told me. In reply he asked mine. The last view I had of him for some time was a hasty retreat through the door of the car for air.

I played my first match against J. C. Parke at Wimbledon in 1920. The time before that I had been on the court with him was at Germantown Cricket Club in 1911, when I acted as ball-boy in the Davis Cup between him and W. A. Larned.

The Junior members of the club, sons of the members, used to consider it a great honour to act as ball-boy in these matches, and worked every means to be picked. I picked up much tennis in those days, for I have worked at the ball-boy position for Parke, Crawley, Dixon, Larned, Wright, and Ward.

CHAPTER IX

THE PSYCHOLOGY OF SINGLES AND DOUBLES

SINGLES, the greatest strain in tennis, is the game for two players. It is in this phase of the game that the personal equation reaches its crest of importance. This is the game of individual effort, mental and physical.

A hard 5-set singles match is the greatest strain on the body and nervous system of any form of sport. Richard Harte and L. C. Wister, the former a famous Harvard University football and baseball player, the latter a football star at Princeton, both of whom are famous tennis players, have told me that a close 5-set tennis match was far more wearing on them than the biggest football game they had ever played.

Singles is a game of daring, dash, speed of foot and stroke. It is a game of chance far more than doubles. Since you have no partner dependent upon you, you can afford to risk error for the possibility of speedy victory. Much of what I wrote under match play is more for singles than doubles, yet let me call your attention to certain peculiarities of singles from the standpoint of the spectator.

A gallery enjoys personalities far more than

styles. Singles brings two people into close and active relations that show the idiosyncrasies of each player far more acutely than doubles. The spectator is in the position of a man watching an insect under a microscope. He can analyse the inner workings.

The freedom of restraint felt on a single court is in marked contrast to the need for team work in doubles. Go out for your shot in singles whenever there is a reasonable chance of getting it. Hit harder at all times in singles than in doubles, for you have more chance of scoring and can take more risk.

Few great singles players are famous in doubles. Notable exceptions to the above statement come to mind at once in the persons of the Dohertys, Norman E. Brookes, and F. B. Alexander. Yet who could accuse W. M. Johnston, R. N. Williams (notwithstanding his World's Championship doubles title), André Gobert, the late Anthony F. Wilding, M. E. M'Loughlin, or Gerald Patterson of playing great doubles? All these men are wonderful singles players, playing singles on a double court alongside some suffering partner. The daring that makes for a great singles player is an eternal appeal to a gallery. None of the notable doubles players, who have little or no claim to singles fame, have enjoyed the hero-worship accorded the famous singles stars. H. Roper-Barrett, Stanley Doust, Harold H. Hackett, Samuel Hardy, and Holcombe Ward, all doubles players of the very highest order, were, and are, well liked and deservedly popular, but are not idolized as were M'Loughlin or Wilding.

Singles is a game of the imagination, doubles a science of exact angles.

Doubles is four-handed tennis. Enough of this primary reader definition. I only used that so as not to be accused of trying to write over the heads of the uninitiated.

It is just as vital to play to your partner in tennis as in bridge. Every time you make a stroke you must do it with a definite plan to avoid putting your partner in trouble. The keynote of doubles success is team work; not individual brilliancy. There is a certain type of team work dependent wholly upon individual brilliancy. Where both players are in the same class, a team is as strong as its weakest player at any given time, for here it is even team work with an equal division of the court that should be the method of play. In the case of one strong player and one weaker player, the team is as good as the strong player can make it by protecting and defending the weaker. This pair should develop its team work on the individual brilliancy of the stronger man.

The first essential of doubles play is to *put the ball in play*. A double fault is bad in singles, but it is inexcusable in doubles. The return of service should be certain. After that it should be low and to the server coming in. Do not strive for clean aces in doubles until you have the opening. Remember that to pass two men is a difficult task.

Always attack in doubles. The net is the only place in the court to play the doubles game, and you should always strive to attain the net position. There are two formations for the receiving team: one is the Australian formation with the receiver's partner standing in to volley the server's return volley; the other is the English and American style with both men back, thus giving the net attack to the server. This is safer, but less likely to produce a winning result unless the team is a wonderful lobbing combination. Lobbing is a sound defence in doubles, and is used to open the court.

I believe in always trying for the kill when you see a real opening. "Poach" (go for a shot which is not really on your side of the court) whenever you see a chance to score. Never poach unless you go for the kill. It is a win or nothing shot since it opens your whole court. If you are missing badly do not poach, as it is very disconcerting to your partner.

The question of covering a doubles court should not be a serious one. With all men striving to attain the net all the time every shot should be built up with that idea. Volley and smash whenever possible, and only retreat when absolutely necessary.

When the ball goes toward the side-line the net player on that side goes in close and toward the line. His partner falls slightly back and to the centre of the court, thus covering the shot between the men. If the next return goes to the other side the two men reverse positions. The theory of court covering is two sides of a triangle, with the angle in the centre and the two sides running to the side-lines and in the direction of the net.

Each man should cover overhead balls over his own head, and hit them in the air whenever possible, since to allow them to drop gives the net to the other team. The only time for the partner to protect the overhead is when the net man "poaches," is outguessed, and the ball tossed over his head. Then the server covers and strives for a kill at once.

Always be ready to protect your partner, but do not take shots over his head unless he calls for you to, or you see a certain kill. Then say "Mine," step in and hit decisively. The matter of overhead balls, crossing under them, and such incidentals of team work are matters of personal opinion, and should be arranged by each team according to their joint views. I only offer general rules that can be modified to meet the wishes of the individuals.

Use the lob as a defence, and to give time to extricate yourself and your partner from a bad position. The value of service in doubles cannot be too strongly emphasized since it gives the net to the server. Service should always be held. To lose service is an unpardonable sin in first-class doubles. All shots in doubles should be low or very high. Do not hit shoulder-high as it is too easy to kill. Volley down and hard if possible. Every shot you make should be made with a definite idea of opening the court.

Hit down the centre to disrupt the team work of the opposing team; but hit to the side-lines for your aces.

Pick one man, preferably the weaker of your opponents, and centre your attack on him and keep it there. Pound him unmercifully, and in time he should crack under the attack. It is very foolish to alternate attack, since it simply puts both men on their game and tires neither.

If your partner starts badly play safely and surely until he rounds to form. Never show annoyance with your partner. Do not scold him. He is doing the best he can, and fighting with him does no good. Encourage him at all times and don't worry. A team that is fighting among themselves has little time left to play tennis, and after all tennis is the main object of doubles.

Offer suggestions to your partner at any time during a match; but do not insist on his following them, and do not get peevish if he doesn't. He simply does not agree with you, and he may be right. Who knows?

Every doubles team should have a leader to direct its play; but that leader must always be willing to drop leadership for any given point when his partner has the superior position. It is policy of attack not type of stroke that the leader should determine.

Pick a partner and stick to him. He should be a man you like and want to play with, and he should want to play with you. This will do away with much friction. His style should not be too nearly your own, since you double the faults without greatly increasing the virtues.

I am a great believer in a brilliant man teaming up with a steady player. Let your steady man keep the ball in play, and allow your brilliant man all the room he wants to "poach" and kill. Thus you get the best of both men.

Doubles is a game of finesse more than speed. The great doubles players, the Dohertys, Norman E. Brookes, the greatest in the world to-day, Roper Barrett, Beals Wright, and F. B. Alexander, are all men of subtle finesse rather than terrific speed.

It requires more than speed of shot to beat two men over a barrier 3 to 3½ feet high with a distance of some 32 feet. It is angles, pace, and accuracy that should be the aim in a great doubles game. Resource, versatility, and subtlety, not speed, win doubles matches.

PART III: MODERN TENNIS AND ITS FUTURE

PART III: MODERN TENNIS AND ITS FUTURE

CHAPTER X

THE GROWTH OF THE MODERN GAME

L AWN tennis is the outgrowth of the old French game of the courts of the early Louis. It spread to England, where it gained a firm hold on public favour. The game divided; the original form being closely adhered to in the game known in America as "Court tennis," but which is called "Tennis" in England. Lawn tennis grew out of it.

The old style game was played over a net some 5 feet high, and the service was always from the same end, the players changing courts each game. It was more on the style of the present game of badminton or battledore and shuttlecock.

Gradually the desire for active play had its effect, in a lowered net and changed laws, and tennis, as we know it, grew into being. From its earliest period, which is deeply shrouded in mystery, came the terms of "love" for "nothing" and "deuce" for "40-all." What they meant originally, or how they gained their hold is unknown, but the terms are a tradition of the game and just as much a part of the scoring system as the "game" or "set" call.

In 1920 the Rules Committee of the American Tennis Association advocated a change in scoring that replaced love, 15, 30, 40 with the more comprehensive 1, 2, 3, 4. The real reason for the proposed change was the belief that the word "love" in tennis made the uninitiated consider the game effeminate and repelled possible supporters. The loyal adherents of the old customs of the game proved too strong, and defeated the proposed change in scoring by an overwhelming majority.

Personally, I think there is some slight claim to consideration for the removal of the word "love." It can do no good, and there are many substitutes for it. It can easily be eliminated without revolutionizing the whole scoring system. It is far easier to substitute the words "zero," "nothing," for "love" than cause such an upheaval as was proposed. In my opinion the best way to obviate the matter is to use the player's name in conjunction with the points won by him, when his opponent has none. If the first point is won by Williams, call the score "15, Williams" and, with his opponent scoring the next, the call would become "15-all."

If tennis loses one adherent, it could otherwise gain, simply by its retaining the word "love" in the score, I heartily advocate removing it. This removal was successfully accomplished in Chicago in 1919, with no confusion to players, umpires, or public.

R. NORRIS WILLIAMS
1914 and in 1916

WILLIAM M. JOHNSTON
1915 and in 1919

MAURICE E. MC LOUGHLIN
1912 and in 1913

ROBERT LINDLEY MURRAY
1917 and in 1918

FORMER CHAMPIONS OF AMERICA

However, returning from my little digression on the relative value of "love" and "nothing," let me continue my short history of the game. The playing of tennis sprang into public favour so quickly that in a comparatively short space of time it was universally played in England and France. The game was brought to America in the latter part of the nineteenth century. Its growth there in the past twenty-five years has been phenomenal. During the last half century tennis gained a firm foothold in all the colonies of the British Empire, and even found favour in the Orient, as is explained in another portion of this book.

Tennis fills many needs of mankind. It provides an outlet for physical energy, relaxation, mental stimulus, and healthful exercise. The moral tone is aided by tennis because the first law of tennis is that every player must be a good sportsman and inherently a gentleman.

Tennis was recognized by the Allied Governments as one of the most beneficial sports during the World War. Not only were the men in service encouraged to play whenever possible, but the Allied Governments lent official aid to the various service tournaments held in France following the signing of the Armistice. The importance of tennis in the eyes of the American Government may be gleaned from the fact that great numbers of hard courts were erected at the various big cantonments, and organized play offered to the soldiers.

Many of the leading players who were in training

in America at the time of the National Championship, which was played solely to raise money for
the Red Cross, were granted leave from their various stations to take part in the competition.
Among the most notable were Wallace F. Johnson,
Conrad B. Doyle, Harold Throckmorton, S. Howard Voshell, and myself, all of whom were granted
leave of two weeks or a month. Captain R. N.
Williams and Ensigns William M. Johnston and
Maurice E. M'Loughlin, and many other stars, were
overseas. Official recognition at such a time puts
a stamp of approval on the game which goes far
to justify its world-wide popularity.

The tennis world lost many of its best in that
titanic struggle. The passing of so many from its
ranks left gaps that will be hard to fill.

The gallant death of Anthony F. Wilding in Flanders cost the game one of its greatest players and
finest men. I had not the pleasure of knowing
Wilding personally yet I, like all the tennis world,
felt a sense of keen personal loss at his heroic
passing. Wilding was a man whose sterling qualities gave even more to the game than his play, and
tennis is better for his all too brief career.

America lost some of its finest manhood in the
War, and tennis paid its toll. No player was a more
likeable personality nor popular figure among the
rising stars than John Plaffman, the young Harvard
man who gave his life in Flanders fields. I cannot
touch on the many heroes who made everlasting
fame in a bigger game than that which they loved

so well. Time is too short. It is sufficient to know that the tennis players of the world dropped their sport at the call of War, and played as well with death as ever they did on the tennis court.

The War is over, please God never to return, and the men are back from their marvellous task. The game of War is done, the games of Peace are again being played. Tennis suffered the world over from war's blight, but everywhere the game sprang up in renewed life at the close of hostilities. The season of 1919 was one of reconstruction after the devastation. New figures were standing in prominence where old stars were accustomed to be seen. The question on the lips of all the tennis players was whether the stars of pre-War days would return to their former greatness.

The Championship of the World for 1919 at Wimbledon was anxiously awaited. Who would stand forth as the shining light of that meeting? Gerald Patterson, the "Australian Hurricane," as the press called him, came through a notable field and successfully challenged Norman Brookes for the title. Gobert and Kingscote fell before him, and the press hailed him as a player of transcendent powers.

The Australian team of Brookes, Patterson, R. V. Thomas, and Randolph Lycett journeyed home to the Antipodes by way of America to compete in the American Championship. Meanwhile R. N. Williams, W. M. Johnston, and Maurice E. M'Loughlin were demobilized, and were again on the courts. The American Championships assumed an importance equal to that of the Wimbledon event.

The Australian team of Brookes and Patterson successfully challenged the American title-holders in doubles, Vincent Richards and myself, after defeating the best teams in America, including W. M. Johnston and C. J. Griffin, the former champions. Speculation was rife as to Patterson's ability to triumph in the Singles Championship, and public interest ran high.

The Singles Championship proved a notable triumph for W. M. Johnston, who won a decisive, clear-cut, and deserved victory from a field never equalled in the history of tennis. Johnston defeated Patterson in a marvellous 5-set struggle, while Brookes lost to me in four sets. M'Loughlin went down to Williams in a match that showed the famous Comet but a faint shadow of his former self. Williams was defeated in sequence sets by me. The final round found Johnston in miraculous form and complete master of the match from start to finish, and he defeated me in three sequence sets.

Immediately following the championship, the Australian-American team match took place. In this Brookes went down to defeat before Johnston in four close sets, while I succeeded in scoring another point by nosing out Patterson by the same score. Thus 1919 gave Johnston a clear claim to the title of the World's Premier Tennis Player.

The whole season saw marked increase in tennis interest throughout the entire world.

I have gone into more detail concerning the season of 1919 than I otherwise would, to attempt to show the revival of the tennis game in the public interest, and why it is so.

The evolution of the tennis game is a natural logical one. There is a definite cycle of events that can be traced. The picture is clearest in America as the steps of advancements are more definitely defined. It is from America that I am going to analyse the growth of modern tennis.

The old saying, "Three generations from shirt sleeves to shirt sleeves," may well be parodied to "Three decades from ground strokes to ground strokes." The game of tennis is one great circle that never quite closes. Progress will not allow a complete return to the old style. Yet the style, without the method of thirty years ago, is coming back in vogue. It is a polished, decorated version of the old type game. It is expanded and developed. History tells us that the civilization of the old Greeks and Romans held many so-called modern luxuries, but not the methods of acquiring them we have to-day. Just so with tennis; for the ground-stroke game was the style of the past, just as it will be the style of the future; but the modern method of making ground strokes is a very different thing from the one used by the old-time stars.

We are on the brink of the upheaval. The next few years will show results in the tennis game that were not thought of before the War. Tennis is becoming an organized sport, with skilled management. Modern methods, where efficiency is the watchword, is the new idea in tennis development.

Tennis is on the verge of the greatest increase in its history. Never before has tennis of all types been so universally played, nor by such great multitudes. Its drawing power is phenomenal, hundreds of thousands of people witnessing matches the world over, and played during the season of 1920.

There are more players of fame now before the public than at any previous time since tennis became established. The standard of play of the masses and quality of game of the stars have risen tremendously in the last decade. No less an authority than Norman E. Brookes, whose active playing days cover a period of twenty years, told me during the American Championships last year at Forest Hills, that in his opinion the game in America had advanced fully "15" in ten years. He stated that he believed the leading players of to-day were the superior of the Larneds, Dohertys, and Pims of the past.

The most remarkable advance has been along the lines of junior play: the development of a large group of boys ranging in age from thirteen to eighteen, who will in time replace the Johnstons, Williams, and M'Loughlins of to-day.

American tennis has passed through a series of revolutionary stages that have changed the complex of the game. English tennis has merely followed its natural development, unaffected by external influences or internal upheaval, so that the game to-day is a refined product of the game of twenty years ago. Refined but not vitalized. The World War alone placed its blight on the English game, and changed the even tenor of its way. Naturally the War had only a devastating effect. No good sprang from it. It is to the everlasting credit of the French and English that during those horrible four years of privation, suffering, and death the sports of the nations lived.

The true type of English tennis, from which American tennis has sprung, was the base-line driving game. It is still the same. Well-executed drives, hit leisurely and gracefully from the baseline, appealed to the temperament of the English people. They developed this style to a perfection well-nigh invincible to cope with from the same position. The English gave the tennis world its traditions, its Dohertys and its Smiths.

Tennis development, just as tennis psychology, is largely a matter of geographical distribution. This is so well recognized now in America that the country is divided in various geographic districts by the national association, and sectional associations carry on the development of their locality under the supervision of the national body.

Naturally new countries, with different customs, would not develop along the same lines as England. America, Australia, and South Africa took the English style, and began their tennis career on the base-line game. Each of these has since had a distinct yet similar growth—a variance to the original style.

American tennis followed the English base-line style through a period that developed Dr. Dwight, R. D. Sears, Henry Slocum, and other stars. Tennis, during this time, was gaining a firm hold among the boys and young men who found the deep-driving game devoid of the excitement they desired. Americans always enjoy experiments, so the rising players tried coming to the net at any reasonable opening. Gradually this plan became popular, until Dwight Davis and Holcombe Ward surprised the tennis world with their new service, now the American twist, and used it as an opening gun in a net attack.

This new system gave us besides Davis and Ward, the Wrenn brothers, George and Robert, Malcolm Whitman, M. G. Chace, and finally Beals C. Wright. The base-line game had its firm adherents who followed it loyally, and it reached its crest in the person of William A. Larned. Previous to this time, speed, cyclonic hitting and furious smashing were unknown, although rumours of some player named M'Loughlin combining these qualities were floating East from the Pacific Coast. Not much stock was taken in this phenomenon until 1908, when Maurice Evans M'Loughlin burst upon the tennis world with a flash of brilliancy that earned him his popular nickname, "The California Comet."

M'Loughlin was the turning-point in American tennis. He made a lasting impression on the game that can never be erased. His personality gained him a following and fame, both in America and England, that have seldom been equalled in the sporting world.

M'Loughlin was the disciple of speed. Cyclonic, dynamic energy, embodied in a fiery-headed boy, transformed tennis to a game of brawn as well as brains. America went crazy over "Red Mac," and all the rising young players sought to emulate his game. No man has brought a more striking personality, or more generous sportsmanship, into tennis than M'Loughlin. The game owes him a great personal debt; but this very personal charm that was his made many players strive to copy his style and methods, which unfortunately were not fundamentally of the best. M'Loughlin was a unique tennis player. His whole game was built up on service and overhead. His ground strokes were very faulty. By his personal popularity M'Loughlin dwarfed the importance of ground strokes, and unduly emphasized the importance of service. M'Loughlin gave us speed, dash, and verve in our tennis. It remained for R. N. Williams and W. M. Johnston to restore the balance of the modern game by solving the riddle of the Californian's service. Brookes and Wilding led the way by first meeting the ball as it came off the ground. Yet neither of these two wizards of the court successfully handled M'Loughlin's service as did Williams and Johnston.

M'Loughlin swept Brookes and Wilding into the discard on those memorable days in 1914, when the dynamic game of the fiery-headed Californian rose to heights it had never attained previously, and he defeated both men in the Davis Cup. Less than one month later Williams, playing as only Williams can, annihilated that mighty delivery and crushed M'Loughlin in the final of the National Championship. It was the beginning of the end for M'Loughlin, for once his attack was repulsed he had no sound defence to fall back on.

Williams and then Johnston triumphed by the wonderful ground strokes that held back M'Loughlin's attack.

To-day we are still in the period of service and net attack, with the cycle closing toward the ground-stroke game. Yet the circle will never close, for the net game is the final word in attack, and only attack will succeed. The evolution means that the ground stroke is again established as the only modern defence against the net player.

Modern tennis should be an attacking service, not necessarily epoch-making, as was M'Loughlin's, but powerfully offensive, with the main portion of the play from the base-line in sparring for openings to advance to the net. Once the opening is made the advance should follow quickly, and the point ended by a decisive kill. That is the modern American game. It is the game of Australia as typified by Patterson schooled under the Brookes tutelage. It is the game of France, played by Gobert, Laurentz, and Brugnon. It has spread to South Africa, and is used by Winslow, Norton, and Raymond. Japan sees its possibilities, and Kumagae and Shimidzu are even now learning the net attack to combine with the base-line game. England alone remains obstinate in her loyalty to her old standby, and even there signs of the joint attack are found in the game of Kingscote.

Tennis has spread so rapidly that the old idea of class and class game has passed away with so many other ancient, yet snobbish, traditions. Tennis is universally played. The need of proper development of the game became so great in America that the American Lawn Tennis Association organized, in 1917, a system of developing the boys under eighteen years of age all over the United States.

The fundamental idea in the system, which had its origin in the able brain of Julian S. Myrick, President of the United States Lawn Tennis Association, was to arouse and sustain interest in the various sections by dealing with local conditions. This was successfully done through a system of local open tournaments, that qualified boys to a sectional championship. These sectional championships in turn qualified the winners for the National Junior Championship, which is held annually in conjunction with the men's event at Forest Hills.

The success of the system has been stupendous. The growth of tennis in certain localities has been phenomenal. In Philadelphia alone over 500 boys compete in sanctioned play annually, while the city ranking for 1919 contained the names of 88 boys under eighteen, and 30 under fifteen, all of whom had competed in at least three sanctioned events.

The school leagues of the city hold a schedule of 726 individual matches a year. The success of the Philadelphia junior system is due to the many large clubs who give the use of their courts and the balls for an open tournament. Among these clubs are Germantown Cricket Club, Cynwyd Club, Philadelphia Cricket, Overbrook Golf Club, Belfield Country Club, Stenton A. C., Green Point Tennis Club, and at times Merion Cricket Club. The movement has been fostered and built up by the efforts of a small group of men, the most important of whom is Paul W. Gibbons, President of the Philadelphia Tennis Association, together with Wm. H. Connell of Germantown, the late Hosmer W. Hanna of Stenton, whose untiring efforts aided greatly in obtaining a real start, Dr. Chuton A. Strong, President of the Interscholastic League, Albert L. Hoskins, for years Vice-President of the U.S.L.T.A., and others. This plan brought great results. It developed such players as Rodney M. Beck, H. F. Domkin, G. B. Pfingst, Carl Fischer, the most promising boy in the city, who has graduated from the junior age limit, and Charles Watson (third), who, in 1920, is the Philadelphia Junior Champion, and one of the most remarkable players for a boy of sixteen I have ever seen.

New York City was fortunate in having F. B. Alexander, the famous Internationalist, to handle the junior tennis there. He, together with Julian S. Myrick, and several other men, built up a series of tournaments around New York that produced some remarkable young players. It is largely due to the junior system that Vincent Richards has become the marvellous player that he is, at such an early age. Second only to Richards, and but a shade behind, are Harold Taylor and Cecil Donaldson, who have just passed out of the junior age limit. Charles Wood, the Indoor Boys Champion, is a remarkable youngster.

In New England, particularly in Providence, through the efforts of J. D. E. Jones, junior tennis is rapidly assuming an important place, and many young stars who will be heard of in the future are coming to the fore. By a strange coincidence the list is headed by the two sons of Jones. They seem to have inherited their father's ability. Arnold W. Jones, the National Boy Champion, is a player of marked ability, with a fine all-around game. Following closely on his heels come J. D. E. Jones, Jr., and Wm. W. Ingraham. From the South one finds John E. Howard. Around Chicago a group of men, led by Samuel Hardy, captain of the 1920 Davis Cup team, and assisted by R. T. Van Arsdale, built up a magnificent system of tournaments and coaching. Hardy left Chicago and came to New York in 1919; but the work which he so ably organized will continue under the supervision of the Western Association. The leading juniors developed in Chicago were Lucian Williams and the Weber brothers, James and Jerry.

From the Pacific Coast, the pioneer in junior development, wonderful boys are continually coming

East. A boy's tennis game matures early in California. M'Loughlin was about eighteen when he first came East; Johnston less than twenty-one when he won the national title the first time; Mervin Griffin and Morgan Fottrell are in 1920 the leading youngsters in California.

The success of the Californians is due largely to the efforts of Dr. Sumner Hardy, brother of Samuel Hardy, and one of the most remarkable figures in the tennis world. Dr. Hardy practically carries the California Association single handed. He is a big factor in American tennis success.

From up in Washington State, a fine young player, Marshall Allen, has come to the fore.

Charles S. Garland, the Davis Cup star, is a former Junior Champion of America, and a product of the junior system in Pittsburg, which is so ably handled by his father, Charles Garland. Other young stars developing include George Moreland and Leonard Reed.

Most of the foregoing is irrelevant, I suppose, but I have gone into detail because I want to prove that America has gone into the matter of junior developments, carefully, systematically, and has produced results.

It has been proved conclusively that it is in the schools that the most favourable progress could be made. Once tennis is placed on the basis of importance it deserves, the boys will take it up. At present there is a tendency to discount tennis and golf in school. This is a big mistake, as these two games are the only ones that a man can play regularly after he leaves college and enters into business. The school can keep a sport alive. It is schools that kept cricket alive in England, and lack of scholastic support that killed it in America. The future of tennis in England, France, Australia, Japan, etc., rests in the hands of the boys. If the game is to grow, tennis must be encouraged among the youngsters and played in the schools.

England is faced with a serious problem. Eton and Harrow, the two big schools, are firm set against tennis. The other institutions naturally follow in the lead of these famous schools. The younger generation is growing up with little or no knowledge of tennis. One thing that forcibly bore in on my mind, during my trip in 1920, was the complete absence of boys of all ages at the various tournaments. In America youngsters from ten years of age up swarm all over the grounds at big tennis events. I saw very few of either at Queen's Club, Wimbledon, Eastbourne, or Edgbaston where I played. The boys do not understand tennis in England, and naturally do not care to play it.

The English Lawn Tennis Association is very desirous of building up tennis in the schools; but so far has not yet succeeded in breaking down the old prejudice. It is really a question of life or death with English tennis at this time. Major A. R. F. Kingscote, the youngest of the leading players in England, is older than any man in the American First ten, with the single exception of Walter T.

Hayes. J. C. Parke has stated definitely that 1920 marked his retirement from the game. He is just under forty. Young players must be found to replace the waning stars. The danger is not immediate, for all the players who proved so good in 1920 seemed certain of several more years of first-class play; but what of the next ten years?

The future development of tennis is dependent largely upon the type of court that will become the standard. All big fixtures to-day are played on grass wherever possible. There is little question but that the grass game is the best. In the first place, it is the old-established custom, and should be maintained i. possible. Secondly, the game is more skilful and more interesting on turf. Thirdly, grass is far easier on the eyes and feet of the players than any other surface.

There are drawbacks to grass courts. Grass cannot grow in all climates. The grass season opens late and closes early. The expense of upkeep is very great, and skilled groundsmen are required at all clubs that have grass courts.

The hard court of clay or dirt, cinder, en-tout-cas, or asphalt allows more continuous play and uniform conditions in more kinds of weather. The bound is truer and higher, but the light and surface are harder on the player. The balls wear light very rapidly, while racquets wear through quite soon.

The advantages are a much longer season on hard courts, with less chance of weather interrupting im-

AN ECHO OF THE WAR
Julian S. Myrick, president U. S. L. T. A.; N. W. Niles, runner-up; Walter Camp, Director of athletics; E. F. Torrey, ex-Vice President U. S. L. T. A. and R. L. Murray, winner at the Patriotic Championship, 1917.

DAVIS CUP DOUBLES TEAM, 1913
M. E. McLoughlin and H. H. Hackett.

FRIENDLY ENEMIES
Ichiya Kumagae and Vincent Richards

portant meetings. The courts reauire far less care in upkeep than grass.

What has been the actual tendency in the last decade? In America the hard courts erected have been approximately nine to one grass. America is rapidly become a hard-court country. France is entirely on a hard-court basis; there are no grass courts at all. Play in South Africa is entirely on hard courts. Australia and the British Isles have successfully repelled the hard-court invasion thus far, although during the past two years the number of hard courts put up in England has exceeded grass.

The en-tout-cas court of peculiar red surface is the most popular composition in England and the Continent.

There seems little doubt but that the hard court is the coming surface in the next decade. Grass will continue to be used for the most important events, but the great majority of the tennis played, exclusive of the championships, will be on hard courts.

The result on the game will be one of increasing the value of the ground stroke and partially cutting down the net attack, since the surface of a hard court is slippery and tends to make it hard to reach the net to volley. Thus the natural attack will become a drive and not a volley. Hard-court play speeds up the ground strokes, and makes the game more orthodox.

The installation of hard courts universally should spread tennis rapidly, since it will afford more chance to play over a longer period. The growth of public courts in the parks and the municipal play grounds in America has been a big factor in the spread of the game's popularity. Formerly a man or boy had to belong to a club in order to have an opportunity to play tennis. Now all he needs is a racquet and balls, and he may play on a public court in his own city. This movement will spread, not only in America but throughout the world. England and France have some public courts; but their systems are not quite as well organized as the American.

The branch of tennis which England and France foster, and in which America is woefully lax, is the indoor game. Unfortunately the majority of the courts abroad have wood surfaces, true but lightning fast. The perfect indoor court should retain its true bound, but slow up the skid of the ball. The most successful surface I have ever played upon is battleship linoleum—the heavy covering used on men-of-war. This gives a true, slightly retarded bound, not unlike a very fast grass court.

Indoor play in America is sadly crippled by reason of no adequate facilities for play. The so-called National Indoor Championship is held at the Seventh Regiment Armoury in New York City on a wood floor, with such frightful lighting that it is impossible to play real tennis. The two covered courts at Longwood Club, Boston, are very fine, well lighted, with plenty of space. There is a magnificent court at Providence, and another at Buffalo. Utica boasts of another, while there are several fine courts, privately owned, on Long Island. New York City uses the big armouries for indoor play; but the surface and light in these are not fit for real tennis. The Brooklyn Heights Casino has the only adequate court in the Metropolitan district.

Philadelphia and Chicago, cities of enormous populations and great tennis interest, have no courts or facilities for indoor play. This condition must be rectified in America if we wish to keep our supremacy in the tennis world. The French players are remarkable on wood. Gobert is said to be the superior of any player in the world, when playing under good conditions indoors. The game of tennis is worthy of having all types of play within reach of its devotees. Why should a player drop his sport in October because the weather is cold? Indoor play during the winter means an improvement from season to season. Lack of it is practically stagnation or retrogression.

The future will see a growth of hard-court play the world over. Grass must fight to hold its position. Indoor play will come more and more into vogue.

CHAPTER XI

THE PROBABLE FUTURE OF THE GAME

WHAT will be the outcome of the world-wide boom in tennis? Will the game change materially in the coming years? Time, alone, can answer; but with that rashness that seizes one when the opportunity to prophesy arrives and no one is at hand to cry "Hold, hold," I dare to submit my views on the coming years in international tennis.

I do not look to see a material change in the playing rules. A revival of the footfault fiend, who desires to handicap the server, is international in character and, like the poor, "always with us." The International Federation has practically adopted a footfault rule for 1921 that prohibits the server lifting one foot unless replaced behind the base-line. It is believed this will do away with the terrific services. The only effect I can see from it is to move the server back a few inches, or possibly a foot, while he delivers the same service and follows in with a little more speed of foot. It will not change the game at all. Sir Oliver Lodge, the eminent scientist, has joined the advocates of but one service per point. This seems so radical and in all so useless, since it entirely kills service as other than a mere formality, and puts it back where it was twenty-five years ago, that I doubt if even the weight of Sir Oliver Lodge's eminent opinion can put it over. To allow one service is to hand the game more fully into the receiver's hands than it now rests in the server's.

The playing rules are adequate in every way, and the perfect accord with which representatives of the various countries meet and play, happily, successfully, and what is more important, annually, is sufficient endorsement of the fundamental principles. The few slight variations of the different countries are easily learned and work no hardships on visiting players. Why change a known successful quantity for an unknown? It seldom pays.

The style of play is now approaching a type which I believe will prove to have a long life. To-day we are beginning to combine the various styles in one man. The champion of the future will necessarily need more equipment than the champion of to-day. The present shows us the forehand driving of Johnston, the service of Murray, the volleying of Richards, the chop of Wallace F. Johnson, the smash of Patterson, the half volley of Williams, and the back hand of Pell. The future will find the greatest players combining much of these games. It can be done if the player will study. I believe that every leading player in the world in 1950 will have a drive and a chop, fore- and backhand from the base-line. He will use at least two styles of service, since one will not suffice against the stroke of that period. He will be a volleyer who can safely advance to the net, yet his attack will be based on a ground game. He must smash well. In short, I believe that the key to future tennis success lies in variety of stroke. The day of the one-stroke player is passing. Each year sees the versatile game striding forward by leaps and bounds.

The future champion of the world must be a man of keen intellect, since psychology is assuming the importance that is its due. He must train earnestly, carefully, and consistently. The day of playing successful tennis and staying up till daybreak is over. The game is too fast and too severe for that. As competition increases the price of success goes up; but its worth increases in a greater ratio, for the man who triumphs in the World's Championship in 1950 will survive a field of stars beyond our wildest dreams in 1920.

What of the various countries? America should retain her place at or near the top, for the boys we are now developing should not only make great players themselves, but should carry on the work of training the coming generations.

England has but to interest her youth in the game to hold her place with the leaders. I believe it will be done. I look to see great advances made in tennis among the boys in England in the next few years. I believe the game will change to conform more to the modern net attack. England will never be the advanced tennis-playing country that her colonies are, for her whole atmosphere is one of conservatism in sport. Still her game will change. Already a slight modification is at work. The next decade will see a big change coming over the style of English tennis. The wonderful sporting abilities of the Englishman, his ability to produce his best when seemingly down and out mean that, no matter how low the ebb to which tennis might fall, the inherent abilities of the English athlete would always bring it up. I sound pessimistic about the immediate future. I am not, provided English boyhood is interested in the game.

Japan is the country of the future. There is no more remarkable race of students on the globe than the Japanese. They like tennis, and are coming with increasing numbers to our tournaments. They prove themselves sterling sportsmen and remarkable players. I look to see Japan a power in tennis in the next twenty-five years.

France, with her brilliant temperamental unstable people, will always provide interesting players and charming opponents. I do not look to see France materially change her present position—which is one of extreme honour, of great friendliness, and keen competition. Her game will not greatly rise, nor will she lose in any way the prestige that is hers.

It will be many long years before the players of those enemy countries, who plunged the world into the horrible baptism of blood from which we have only just emerged, will ever be met by the players of the Allies. Personally, I trust I may not see their re-entry into the game. Not from the question of the individuals, but from the feeling which will not down. There is no need to deal at this time with the future of Germany and Austria.

Australasia and South Africa, the great colonies of the British Empire, should be on the edge of a great tennis wave. I look to see great players rise in Australasia to refill the gaps left by the passing of Wilding and the retirement of Brookes. It takes great players to fill such gaps; but great players are bred from the traditions of the former masters.

The early season of 1921 saw a significant and to my way of looking at it, wise move on the part of New Zealand when the New Zealand tennis association withdrew from the Australasian tennis association and decided to compete for the Davis Cup in future years as a separate nation.

No one can deny the great help Australia has been to New Zealand in tennis development, but the time has come now for New Zealand to stand on her own. Since the regrettable death of Anthony F. Wilding, in whose memory New Zealand has a tennis asset and standard that will always hold a place in world sport, the New Zealand tennis players have been unable to produce a player of skill enough to make the Davis Cup team of Australasia. It has fallen to Australia with Norman E. Brookes, to whose unfailing support and interest Australasian tennis owes its progress since the war, G. L. Patterson, W. H. Anderson, R. L.

Heath, and Pat O'Hara Wood to uphold the traditions of the game.

The Davis Cup cnallenge round of 1921 was staged in New Zealand in accord with the agreement between Australia and New Zealand and also in memory of A. F. Wilding. The tremendous interest in the play throughout the entire country showed the time was ripe for a drastic step forward if the step was ever to be taken. So after careful consideration the split of Australia and New Zealand has taken place. What will this mean to New Zealand? First it means that it will be years before another Davis Cup match will be staged on her shores, for it takes time and plenty of it to produce a winning team, but at the time, the fact is borne in on the tennis playing faction in New Zealand that as soon as they desire to challenge, their players will gain the opportunity of International competition.

Experience matures players faster than anything else and I am sure that the move that will place a team of New Zealand players in the field in the Davis Cup will be the first and biggest step forward to real world power in tennis. New Zealand produced one Wilding, why should not another appear?

I was tremendously impressed by the interest existing among the New Zealand boys in tennis. I met a great number during my few weeks in Auckland and seldom have seen such a magnificent physical type coupled with mental keenness. These boys, given the opportunity to play under adequate supervision and coaching, should produce tennis players of the highest class.

The New Zealand association has made a drastic move. I hope they have the wisdom to see far enough ahead to provide plenty of play for their young players and if possible to obtain adequate coaches in the clubs and schools.

Frankly I see no players of Davis Cup calibre now in New Zealand. I did see many boys whom I felt if given the chance would become Davis Cup material.

The break with New Zealand will have no effect on Australia, except to relieve a slight friction that has existed. Australia has plenty of material coming to insure a succession of fine teams for the Davis Cup in the future.

Both Australia and New Zealand handle their tennis in the country in a most efficient manner and the game seems to me to be progressing in a natural and healthy manner. The next ten years will decide the fate of New Zealand tennis. If they organise a systematic development of their boys I feel convinced they will gain a place of equality with Australia. If they do not seize their opening now, tennis will not revive until some genius of the game such as Norman E. Brookes arises in their midst from only the Lord knows where.

The future should see America and Australia fighting for supremacy in the tennis world, with

England and France close on their heels, to jump in the lead at the first faltering.

It is only a matter of time before the last differences between the International Federation and the America Association are patched up. The fundamental desires of each, to spread the growth of tennis, are the same. Sooner or later the bar will fall, and a truly International Federation, worldwide in scope, will follow.

I look to see the Davis Cup matches gain in importance and public interest as each year goes by. The growth of the public interest in the game is seen at every hand. Wimbledon must seek new quarters. The new grounds of the All England Club will provide accommodation for 20,000 to witness the championships. This enormous stadium is the result of public pressure, owing to the crowds that could not be accommodated at the old grounds.

Westside Club, Forest Hills, where the American Championship was held, is planning accommodation for 25,000, provided that they are awarded the championship for a long term of years. Davis Cup matches are now drawing from 10,000 to 15,000 where the accommodation is available. What will the future hold?

I believe that 1950 will find the game of tennis on a plane undreamed of to-day. Tennis is still in its infancy. May I have the pleasure to help in rocking the cradle.

My task is completed. I have delved into the past, analysed the present, and prophesied the future, with a complete disregard of conventions and traditions.

The old order changeth, and I trust that my book may aid slightly in turning the tennis thought in the direction of organized developments. The day of self is past. The day of co-operation is dawning. It is seen in the junior tennis, the municipal tennis, and the spirit of international brotherhood in the game.

Assistance is necessary to success in any venture. My book has been made possible only by the aid afforded me by several of my companions on the Davis Cup team trip. The task of arranging the material in coherent order and proper style is one of the most important points. I owe a debt of gratitude to Mrs. Samuel Hardy, wife of our captain, for her never-failing interest and keen judgment in the matter of style.

Mr. Hardy, with his great knowledge of the game of tennis, as player, official, and organizer, freely gave of his store of experience, and to him I owe much that is interesting in the tactics of the game.

R. N. Williams, my team-mate, was always a willing critic and generous listener, and his playing abilities and decided ideas on the game gave much material that found its way into these pages. I wish to express my gratitude for his able assistance.

Charles S. Garland, my doubles partner and close friend, gave never-wavering faith and a willing ear to my ravings over strokes, tactics, and theories,

while his orthodox views on tennis acted as a stop
on my rather Bolshevik ideas.

To all these people I express my thanks for their
part in any success I may attain with this book. I
have a firm belief in the future of tennis. I recommend it to all. It gives firm friends, a healthy body,
a keen mind, and a clean sport. It calls forth the
best that is in you, and repays you in its own coin.

THE 1921 SEASON

The season of 1921 was the most remarkable
year in tennis history throughout the whole world.
More tennis was played and more people viewed it
than ever before.

The climax of famous Davis Cup competition
was reached when England, France, Japan, Australia, the Philippines, Denmark, Belgium, Argentine, Spain, India, Canada and Czecho-Slovakia challenged for the right to play America, the holding
nation. This wonderful representation naturally
produced not only many new stars, but also thousands of new enthusiasts in the various countries
where the matches were played.

The early rounds saw several brilliant matches
and naturally some defaults. Argentine and the
Philippines could not put a team in the field at the
last moment. Belgium, after defeating Czecho-Slovakia, was unable to finance her team to America
to meet the winner of England and Australasia.

England scored a fine victory over Spain when
Randolph Lycett, F. Gordon Lowe and Max E.

Woosnam defeated Manuel Alonzo and Count de Gomar in a close meeting. Notwithstanding his defeat by Lycett, Manuel Alonzo proved himself one of the great players of the world and one of the most attractive personalities in tennis.

India sprang a sensation by defeating France in their match in Paris. Sleen, Jacob and Deane showed great promise for the future. France was crippled owing to the loss of A. H. Gobert and William Laurentz, the former through a seriously sprained ankle sustained in the World's Championship at Wimbledon, and the latter through illness. Samazieuhl, the new French champion, and Brugnon could not cope with the steadiness of the Indian stars and the team from the Orient won 3 matches to 2. Meanwhile the Australian team of J. O. Anderson, J. B. Hawkes, C. V. Todd and Norman Peach had arrived in America and journeyed to Canada, where they swamped their Colonial cousins easily. Norman E. Brookes, Gerald L. Patterson and Pat O'Hara Wood were unable to accompany the team, so the greatest contender for the title was weakened appreciably.

The Australians decisively defeated the Danish team of Tegner and Van Ingersley at Cleveland, winning with ease. They proceeded to Pittsburgh to await the arrival of the English players.

England sent her invading team, unfortunately without the services of Col. A. R. F. Kingscote and Randolph Lycett, who were unable to go owing to business affairs. J. C. Parke, her famous interna-

tional star, was also out of the game, having retired from active competition last year. The English team was made up of Gordon Lowe, Max
Woosnam, J. C. Gilbert and O. E. H. Turnbull.
They were accompanied by that delightful author
and critic A. Wallis Meyers.

The English met the Australians at Pittsburgh
in July. The latter won three matches to two with
J. O. Anderson, the outstanding figure of a well
played meeting. The tall Australian defeated both
Lowe and Woosnam in the singles and aided in the
doubles victory, thus scoring all the points for his
team.

Meanwhile the Indian team had arrived in America and proceeded to Chicago, where they met the
Japanese team of Kumagae and Shimidzu. The
battle of the Orient resulted in a victory for the
Nipponese.

The final round found Australia playing Japan in
the famous old tennis center of Newport, R. I.,
where the National Singles so long held sway. It
was a bitter struggle, with the Australians within
two little points of victory in two matches they
afterwards lost. Shimidzu and Kumagae took all
the singles, but Kumagae was two sets down to
Hawkes and one to two down to Anderson. Thus
Japan in its first year in Davis Cup competition
earned the right to challenge America for the treas-
ured trophy.

It was a marvellous meeting of these two teams.
Over 40,000 people watched the players in three

days.   Although America won all five matches, Shimidzu came within two points of defeating me in straight sets and carried Johnston to a bitter four set struggle.

The Cup is safe for another year but the new blood infused into the competition by such men as Shimidzu, Alonzo, Woosnam, Anderson and Hawkes shows clearly that America must keep working or we will fall from our present position. It is a healthy thing for the game that this is so. I hope we will see many more new players of equal promise next year.

The United States Lawn Tennis Association, following its policy of co-operation with the International Federation, decided to send a team to France and England for the championships.   The personnel of the team was Mrs. Franklin I. Mallory, Miss Edith Sigourney, Arnold W. Jones (boy champion of America, 1919), and myself.   J. D. E. Jones, father of Arnold, himself a tennis player of renown, accompanied the team, as did Mr. Mallory.

The invading tennis players sailed May 12th on the *Mauretania* to Cherbourg and from there journeyed to Paris, where they engaged in the Hard Court Championship of the world.

The first week of the stay was devoted to practice on the courts at the Stad Français, St. Cloud, where the championship was held.   The team were the guests of the Racing Club at a most delightful luncheon and shortly afterward dined as the guests of the Tennis Club of Paris.

WALLACE F. JOHNSTON
America

S. HOWARD VOSHELL
America

ICHIYA KUMAGAE
Japan

WATSON M. WASHBURN
America

The finals of the championship of France were held during our stay and, greatly to our surprise, A. H. Gobert, the defending title holder, fell a victim to his old enemy, heat, and went down to defeat before Samazieuhl. The Hard Court championships of the world produced a series of the most sensational upsets in the history of the game, a series, I might add, that did much to allow me to win the event. Gobert lost to Nicholas Mishu in the first round. Alonzo, after defeating Samazieuhl, went down to defeat at hands of Laurentz, who in turn collapsed to Tegner. Fate pursued the winners, for Tegner was eliminated by Washer, who came through to the final against me. Either Alonzo or Laurentz should have been finalists if the unexpected had not occurred, and either would have been a hard proposition for me particularly in my condition. I had been taken ill on my arrival in Paris and was still far from well. However, Fortune smiled on me and I succeeded in defeating Washer 6–3, 6–3, 6–3.

Meanwhile the long awaited meeting between Mlle. Lenglen and Mrs. Mallory was at hand. Mrs. Mallory had come through one side of the tournament after a bitter battle with Mme. Billoutt (Mlle. Brocadies) in the semi final.

Mlle. Lenglen had proceeded in her usual leisurely fashion to the finals with the loss of but two games.

What a meeting these two great players, Mrs. Mallory and Mlle. Lenglen, had! Every seat in the stands sold and every inch of standing room crowded! It was a marvellous match, both women playing great tennis. Mlle. Lenglen had consistently better depth and more patience. She outmanœuvred the American champion and won 6–2, 6–3. The match was far closer than this one-sided score sounds. Every rally was long drawn out and bitterly contested, but the French girl had a slight superiority that brought her a well deserved victory.

A. H. Gobert and W. Laurentz retained their doubles title after one of the most terrific struggles of their careers in the semi-final round against Arnold Jones and me. The boy and I had previously put out Samazieuhl and his partner in three sets and just nosed out the Spanish Davis Cup team, Manuel Alonzo and Count de Gomar.

The semi final between Gobert and Laurentz and the Americans brought out a capacity audience that literally jumped to its feet and cheered during the sparkling rallies of the five bitterly contesting sets. Just as Gobert drove his terrific service ace past me for the match, Laurentz suddenly collapsed and fainted dead away on the court. It was a dramatic end to a sensational match.

The scene then shifted to England, where the American team journeyed across the Channel to prepare for the Grass Court championship of the world at Wimbledon. My preparation consisted of a hasty journey to a hospital, where a minor operation put me to bed until the day Wimbledon started.

The remainder of the team journeyed first to Beckenham and then to Roehampton for their first grass court play of the season. Mrs. Mallory met defeat at the hands of Mrs. Beamish at Beckenham while the other members fell by the wayside at sundry points. Mrs. Mallory won Roehampton, decisively defeating Miss Phillis Howkins in the final. Francis T. Hunter, another American who joined the team in England, although he was abroad on business, scored a victory in the men's event at Roehampton.

The world's championship at Wimbledon was another series of sensational matches and startling upsets. The draw as usual was topheavy, all the strength in the upper half with Frank Hunter and B. I. C. Norton in the lower. Every day saw its feature matches produce the unexpected. Shimidzu and Lycett battled for nearly four hours in a struggle that combined all the virtues and vices of tennis and pugilism. Col. A. R. F. Kingscote, after three sensational victories over Fisher, Dixon and Lowe, collapsed against Alonzo and was decisively defeated. Shimidzu looked a certain winner against Alonzo when he led at 2 sets to 1 and 4–1, but the Spaniard rose to great heights and by sensational play pulled out the match in five sets.

Norton and Hunter, after several close calls, met in the semi final. Norton took two sets and led 5–3 in the third only to have Hunter follow in Alonzo's footsteps and pull out the set and win the next. Here Norton again took command and ran out the match.

The Norton-Alonzo match in the final round was a sensational reversal. The Spaniard seemed assured of victory when he took two sets and led at 5–3 and 30-all, but the last-minute jinx that pursued the tournament fell upon him, for Norton came to life and, playing sensational tennis, pulled out the match and earned the right to me in the challenge round.

Then the jinx arose again and this time Babe Norton was the victim. Such a match as that challenge round produced! I went on the court feeling far from well and very much run down. Babe was on the crest but very nervous. He ran away with the first two sets with great ease. The third set I improved. Babe, after dropping three games, decided to let it go. The fourth set found the crowd excited and rather noisy. Norton became annoyed because he felt I was bothered, and he blew up. He simply threw away the fourth set from sheer nerves.

The fifth set was terrible. Norton had come to earth and was playing well while I for the first time in the match had some control of the ball. Norton finally led at 4–5 and 30–40 on my service, with the championship one point away.

We had a long rally. Desperately I hit down the line. I was so certain my shot was going out I started for the net to shake hands. The ball fell on the line and Babe in the excitement of the moment put his return out by inches. It was a life and fortunately for me I seized my chance and succeeded in pulling out the match and retaining the championship. Norton deserved to win, for nothing but luck saved me as I walked to the net, thinking my shot was out. Norton is the youngest man to have won the All Comers Singles. He is just 21.

The championships had two sad moments. One was the absence of J. C. Parke, due to retirement from singles. The other was the retirement of A. W. Gore, the famous veteran, after 30 years a participant in the championships.

The women's events found an even more unfortunate draw than the men. All the strength was in one eight. Miss Ryan defeated Miss K. McKane in the first round and Mrs. Beamish her old rival in the second. She met Mrs. Mallory in the third.

For one set Mrs. Mallory played the finest tennis of her career to that time and in fact equal even to her play against Suzanne Lenglen in America. She ran off six games in ten minutes. Miss Ryan, cleverly changing her game, finally broke up the perfection of Mrs. Mallory's stroking and just nosed her out in the next two sets. It was a well deserved victory.

Miss Ryan easily won the tournament and challenged Mlle. Lenglen, but her old jinx in the form of Suzanne again proved too much and she played far below her best. The French girl easily retained her title, winning 6–2, 6–0.

The journey of the wandering tennis troupe abroad was far from the most important development of the year. The American season was producing remarkable results. Every year produces its outstanding figure and the early months of 1921 saw Vincent Richards looming large on the tennis horizon.

The first sensation of the year was the decisive defeat inflicted on Kumagae by young Richards at Amakassin Club, New York. This was immediately followed by Kumagae's victory over Dick Williams, avenging Williams' win at Palm Beach some months before. Kumagae scored in the intercity match for the George Myers Church Trophy played in 1921 in Philadelphia. The following day Wallace F. Johnson defeated Kumagae in one of the most terrific battle of the year.

Vincent Richards went through the season to the middle of July without sustaining a defeat. He won five tournaments.

I arrived home from France and England July 12th and journeyed at once to Providence where I took charge of the Rhode Island State Championship at the Agawam Hunt Club. Zenzo Shimidzu had accompanied me to America on the *Olympic* and made his first tournament appearance two days after landing at Greenwich, Conn., before coming to Providence. He went down to unexpected defeat at the hands of S. H. Voshell.

The Providence tournament held the greatest entry list of any event except the National Singles itself. The singles had Shimidzu, Williams, Richards, C. S. Garland, Watson Washburn, S. H. Voshell, Samuel Hardy, N. W. Niles, many young Western collegiate stars and myself. Ichiya Kumagae arrived to play doubles with Shimidzu in preparation for the Davis Cup.

Then the fun began. Shimidzu again fell before the net attack of Voshell, who was himself defeated by the calm quiet steadiness of Washburn. Garland went out at my hands. Williams faced certain defeat when Niles led him 4–0 in the final set, but in one of his super-tennis streaks tore through to victory, only to collapse against Vincent Richards and suffer a crushing defeat 6–2, 6–2 in the semi-final. Meanwhile Washburn had dropped by the wayside to me 6–2, 6–2 and young Richards and I took up our annual battle.

Youth is cruel. The world is cruel. Life is hard. I know it, for Vinnie, with care and discretion, quietly led me along the Road of the Has-Beens, where he deposited me to the tune of 6–1, 6–2, 1–6, 6–0.

Richards, with the scalps of Kumagae, Williams, Voshell and myself dangling at his belt, seemed destined for the championship itself. Alas, pride goeth before a fall. The fall came to Vinnie suddenly.

The following week was the Longwood Singles. "Little Bill" Johnston arrived East, together with the rest of his California team, the day the event started. Johnston was the holder of the trophy and was called on to meet the winner of the tournament in the challenge round.

The tournament was mainly Dick Williams. He defeated Shimidzu in the final. Kumagae was his victim in an earlier round.

Willis E. Davis, second string of the California team, was unexpectedly defeated by N. W. Niles, who himself went the long road via Shimidzu. The little Japanese star scored another important victory when he defeated W. F. Johnson.

Williams met Johnston in the challenge round with chances bright. Somehow Little Bill has Dick's number these days and again decisively defeated him. Vincent Richards wisely rested the week of Longwood, preparing for the later events. I was off in the woods at Camp Winnipesaukee recuperating from the effects of illness in England.

Newport followed on the heels of Longwood. Newport should be called Washburn Week. Here the judicial Watty methodically placed Johnston and Williams in the discard on successive days. It was a notable performance.

Williams took an awful revenge on Vinnie Richards when the two met in the third round. It was Williams' day and he blew the little Yonkers boy off the court in one of the finest displays of the whole year. Shimidzu, who had again scored a victory over Wallace Johnson, was taken suddenly ill with ptomaine poisoning, the night before he was to meet Williams in the semi final, and compelled to default. It robbed him of a chance to gain revenge for his defeat at Longwood. Washburn played the best tennis of his life, in defeating Johnston and Williams, which, coupled with Richards' crushing defeat, placed Washburn on the Davis Cup team.

A sensational upset occurred in the first round when L. B. Rice defeated W. E. Davis. Rice has made a great improvement this year and bids fair to go far.

Seabright, the next week, found Little Bill Johnston playing the stellar rôle. Washburn took a week off but Williams and Richards were in the competition.

Johnston crushed Richards when the two met, in a display of aggressive tennis so remarkable that the boy was helpless before it. Richards was stale and below form, but even if he had been at his best, he could not have withstood Johnston's attack. Little Bill followed this up by sweeping Williams off the court by another marvellous streak of well nigh perfect tennis.

Southampton and the Women's National Championship conflicted the next week. The story of Mrs. Mallory's sensational triumph and successful defense of her title is told elsewhere in this book.

Southampton, as always, proved the goat, for almost all the leading players took a week's rest before the National Doubles Championship.

The English Davis Cup team, Willis E. Davis, Vincent Richards and the Kinsey brothers, Bob and Howard, were the leading stars. The event narrowed to Davis and Richards in the finals with no upsets of a startling nature. Davis had had a very poor record all year, while Richards boasted of the finest list of victories of the season. On the other hand the boy was over-tennised and stale and it proved his undoing, for after one set, which he won easily, the sting went out of his game and Davis took the match in four sets.

The championships were just ahead. The Doubles held at Longwood Club, Boston, found several teams closely matched. Williams and Washburn, with the Rhode Island State and Newport to their credit, were the favorites for the title. "Little Bill" Johnston and W. E. Davis and Bob and Howard Kinsey of California had both pressed them closely. Vincent Richards and I teamed together for the first time since N. E. Brookes and G. L. Patterson had won the title from us in 1919. Samuel Hardy and S. H. Voshell were a pair of veterans who needed watching.

Williams and Washburn had a close call in the third round when Hardy and Voshell led 3–1 in the fifth set, but an unfortunate miss of an easy volley by Hardy and a footfault on game point at 3–4 and 30–40 by Voshell turned the tide and the favorites were safe. Johnston and Davis had several chances in the semi-final but Davis was too uncertain and Bill too anxious and they tossed away the opportunities.

Vinnie and I met the Kinseys in the semi-final and after chasing their lobs all over the court for hours and smashing until our backs ached, we finally pulled out three sequence sets. I have seldom seen a team work together more smoothly than the Kinseys.

The final match between Williams and Washburn, Richards and I for two sets was as sensational and closely contested doubles as ever featured a national championship. Our slight superiority in returning service gave us just enough margin to pull out the first two sets 14–12, 12–10. Then Richards went mad. There is no other way to describe it. Every time he got his racquet on a ball it went for a clean placement. I stood around and watched him. Almost single-handed this remarkable boy won the last set 6-2.

The Davis Cup challenge round stretched itself between the Doubles and Singles Championship. There was no work except for us poor hard-working players who were on the team. The rest was a blessing to Richards, who needed it badly, as he was tired and drawn.

Following the American victory in the Davis Cup, the scene shifted to Philadelphia and the eyes of the tennis world were centered on the Germantown Cricket Club, where the greatest tournament of all time was to be held. Players of seven nations were to compete. The Davis Cup stars of England, Australia and Japan added their brilliance to that of all the leading American players. Six American champions, W. A. Larned, W. J. Clothier, R. N. Williams, R. L. Murray, W. M. Johnston, and myself were entered.

Fate took a hand in the draw and for once I think

did so badly that it settled the "blind draw" forever.
In one sixteen Johnston, Richards, Shimidzu, Murray and I were bunched.   The howl of protest from
tennis players and public alike was so loud that the
blind draw surely will go by the board at the coming
annual meeting.   Since the foregoing was written,
the prophecy has proved true.   The annual meeting,
Feb. 4th, 1922, adopted the "Seeded Draw"
unanimously.

Every day produced its thrills, but play ran singularly true to form in most cases.   Illness took a hand
in the game, compelling the defaults of R. L. Murray, Ichiya Kumagae and W. A. Larned.

The early rounds saw but one upset.   Norman
Peach, Captain of the Australasian Davis Cup team,
was eliminated by William W. Ingraham, of Providence, one of the best junior players in America.
It was a splendid victory and shows the fruit our
junior development system is already bearing.   Peach
had not been well but for all that he played a splendid
game and all credit is due Ingraham for his victory.

The second day's play saw a remarkable match
when W. E. Davis defeated C. V. Todd of Australia
after the latter led him by two sets.   Davis steadily
improved and by rushing the net succeeded in breaking up Todd's driving game.   Todd unfortunately
pulled a muscle in his side that seriously hampered
him in the fifth set.

Wallace F. Johnson, playing magnificent tennis,
eliminated Watson Washburn in one of the brainiest,
hardest fought matches of the whole tournament.

Johnson was very steady and outlasted Washburn in the first set, which he won. Washburn then took to storming the net and carried off two sets decisively. The strain took its toll and he was perceptibly slower when the fourth set opened. Johnson ran him from corner to corner, or tossed high lobs when Washburn took the net. It proved too much for even Washburn to stand, and the Philadelphian won the next two sets and with it the match. Many people considered it a great upset. Personally I expected it, as I know how dangerous Johnson may be.

The Johnston-Richards match and my meeting with Shimidzu came on the third day. Fully 15,000 people jammed themselves around the court and yelled, clapped and howled their excitement through the afternoon. It was a splendidly behaved gallery but a very enthusiastic one.

Richards, eager to avenge his crushing defeat by Johnston at Seabright, started with a rush. "Little Bill" was uncertain and rather nervous. Richards ran away with the first two sets almost before Johnston realized what was happening. The tennis Richards played in these sets was almost unbeatable. Johnston nerved himself to his task and held even to 3-all in the third. Here he broke through and Richards, I think foolishly, made little attempt to pull out the set. The boy staked all on the fourth set. Johnston led at 5-3 but Richards, playing desperately, pulled up to 6-5 and was within two points of the match at 30-all on Johnston's service. It was his last effort. Johnston took the game and Richards faded away.   His strength failed him and the match was Johnston's.

I hit a good streak against Shimidzu and ran away with three straight sets more or less easily.

Meantime one of the most sensational upsets of the whole tournament was taking place on an outside court where Stanley W. Pearson of Philadelphia was running the legs off N. W. Niles of Boston and beating him in five sets.

"Little Bill" Johnston and I met the next day in what was the deciding match of the tournament, even though it was only the fourth round.   Every available inch of space was jammed by an overflow gallery when we took the count.   It was a bitter match from the first point.   We were both playing well.   In the early stages Little Bill had a slight edge, but after one set the balance shifted and I held the whip hand to the end.

The same day Dick Williams went down to sudden and unexpected defeat at the hands of J. O. Anderson of Australia in five well played sets.   It was a typical Williams effort, glorious tennis one minute followed by inexcusable lapses.   The Australian was steady and clever throughout.

The keen speculation as to the outcome of the tournament fell off after the meeting of Johnston and I, and with it a decrease in attendance.   This ran very high, however, again reaching capacity on the day of the finals.

The round before the semi finals saw a terrific struggle between two Californians, Bob Kinsey and

Willis E. Davis. Kinsey had defeated Davis in the Metropolitan Championship the week before and was expected to repeat, but Davis managed to outlast his team and nosed out the match. Kinsey collapsed on the court from exhaustion as the last point was played.

Gordon Lowe went down to me in a fine match while J. O. Anderson and Wallace Johnson completed the Quartet of semi finalists.

I finally got my revenge on Davis for the many defeats he had inflicted on me in years gone by. Wallace Johnson scored a magnificent victory over J. O. Anderson in four sets after the Australian led at a set all, 5–2, and 40–15. Johnson ran the visiting Davis Cup star all over the court and finally pulled out the match in one of the finest displays of court generalship I have ever seen.

The finals was more or less of a family party. It was an all-Philadelphian affair, two Philadelphians competing with 14,000 more cheering them on.

Johnson was unfortunate. Saturday the match was started under a dark sky on a soft court that just suited him. I have seldom seen Johnson play so well; as always, his judgment was faultless. We divided games with service with monotonous regularity. The score was 5-all when it began to drizzle. The court, soft at best that day, grew more treacherous and slippery by the minute. Johnson's shots hardly left the ground. He broke my service at 7-all when the rain materially increased. He reached 40–15 but, with the crowd moving to shelter and the rain falling harder every minute, he made the fatal error of hurrying and netted two easy shots for deuce. A moment more and the game was mine and the match called at 8-all.

Play was resumed on Monday before a capacity gallery. By mutual agreement the match was played over from the beginning. I had learned my lesson the previous day and opened with a rush. The hot sun and strong wind had hardened the court and Johnson's shots rose quite high. It was my day and fortunately for me I made the most of it.

I consider that match the best tennis of my life. I beat Johnson 6–1, 6–3, 6–1 in 45 minutes. Thus fell the curtain on the official tennis season.

The East-West matches in Chicago proved more or less of an anti-climax. Johnston was ill and unable to compete, while Wallace Johnson, Williams, Washburn and Shimidzu could not play. Several remarkable matches featured the three days' play in the Windy City. The most remarkable was the splendid victory of J. O. Anderson over me in five sets, the final one of which hung up a world's record for tournament play by going to 19–17. Frank T. Anderson defeated Robert Kinsey in five sets, a splendid performance, while S. H. Voshell scored over W. E. Davis.

The Ranking Committee faces a hard task on the season's play. Let us look at the records of some of the American players, and a few of our visitors.

VINCENT RICHARDS
The greatest Junior player in the
world.

A. L. WIENER (SANDY) AND
WM. T. TILDEN 2ND
Discussing a coming match as they
take the court.

MISS HELEN WILLS
Girl Champion of America

A GROUP OF YOUNG PLAYERS.

CARL FISCHER

C. S. GARLAND AND R. N. WILLIAMS
America

C. HARDY
America

A. G. GOBERT
France

W. A. LAURENTZ
France

1. W. M. Johnston

Beat V. Richards 2, Williams (2), Kumagae, Shimidzu, Roland Roberts, Davis and others. Lost to Washburn, Tilden, Roberts.

2. R. N. Williams 2d.

Beat Richards, Shimidzu, Kumagae (2), Voshell and others. Lost to Johnston (2), Richards, J. O. Anderson, Kumagae.

3. Vincent Richards

Beat Tilden, Richards, Kumagae (2), Shimidzu (2), (in exhibition at Toronto), Voshell, Hawkes, Lost to Johnston (2), Williams, Davis.

4. Ishiya Kumagae

Beat Williams, Voshell, Anderson, Hawkes. Lost to Johnston, Tilden, Williams, Richards.

5. Zenzo Shimidzu

Beat Wallace Johnson (2), Anderson, Hawkes, Niles. Lost to Johnston, Tilden (2), Voshell (2). Richards (2) (in exhibitions).

6. Wallace Johnson

Beat Watson, Washburn, Anderson. Lost to Tilden, Shimidzu (2).

7. Watson Washburn

Beat Williams, Johnston, Voshell. Lost to Wallace Johnson, Tilden, Atherton Richards (a most sensational upset).

8. J. O. Anderson of Australia

Beat R. N. Williams, Tilden, Hawkes, Lowe. Lost to Wallace Johnson, Kumagae, Shimidzu.

9. S. H. Voshell

Beat Shimidzu (2), Davis. Lost to Richards, Williams, Washburn, Neer (an upset), Allen Behr (a gift).

10. W. E. Davis

Beat Richards, R. Kinsey, Lowe. Lost to Niles, L. B. Rice (an upset), R. Kinsey, Voshell and Tilden.

These few records show how useless comparative scores may be. If another season like 1921 strikes American tennis, the ranking will need either clairvoyance or a padded cell.

These upsets are part of the zest of the game and it is due to the very uncertainty of tennis that the public is daily becoming more enthusiastic about the game. I believe next year will see even a greater interest taken in it than was shown this.

Second in importance only to the big events themselves was the season in Junior tennis.

Little Miss Helen Wills, in her first Eastern season, won the Junior championship for girls and brought to the game one of the most delightful personalities that has appeared in many years. Her success at her early age should prove a great boom to girls' tennis all over America.

Vincent Richards passes from the Junior ranks this year but leaves a successor who is worthy to wear his mantle in the person of Arnold W. Jones of Providence. Jones should outclass the field in 1922, by as wide a margin as did Richards this year.

Arnold Jones has had a remarkable record. He won the boys' championship of America in 1919. In 1920 he carried Richards to a close match in the National Junior Singles, taking one set. He was ranked "two" for the year.

This year Arnold had his greatest year of his brief career. He journeyed to France and England, as the official Junior representative of America, recognized by the National Tennis Association. He played splendidly in France, defeating A. Cousin in the hard court championship of the world and forced Tegner, the Danish Davis Cup star, to a close battle before admitting defeat. His sensational play in the doubles was a great aid in carrying him and me to the semi-final ground, where we lost to Gobert and Laurentz after five terrific sets. In England young Jones played Jacob, Captain of the Indian Davis Cup team, a splendid match.

On his return to America he carved his niche in the Hall of Junior Tennis fame by defeating Harold Godshall of California, W. W. Ingraham of Providence and Morgan Bernstein of New York on successive days in the Junior championship. He forced Richards to a bitter fight in final, and again proved beyond question that he is but a step behind Richards today, although he is a full year younger.

Godshall, Ingraham, Charles Wood, Jr., Bernstein, Jerry Lang, Charles Watson III, Fritz Mercur and many other boys are but a step behind Jones. With this list of rising players, need we face the future with anything but the most supreme confidence in our ability to hold our place in the tennis world!

There were two other remarkable features to the tennis season of 1921, both of them in America. The first was the appearance of the Davis Cup team on the court of the White House, Washington, in response to a personal invitation from President and Mrs. Harding. The President, who is a keen sportsman, placed official approval on tennis by this act. On May 8th and 9th, Captain Samuel Hardy, R. N. Williams, Watson Washburn and I, together with Wallace F. Johnson, who understudied for William M. Johnston, met in a series of matches before a brilliant assembly of Diplomatic, Military and Political personages. C. S. Garland was unable to accompany the team owing to illness. Julian S. Myrick, President of the U. S. L. T. A., and A. Y. Leech completed the party.

Rain, that hoodoo of tennis, attempted to ruin the event for it fell steadily for the five days previous to the match. The court was a sea of mud on the morning scheduled, but the President desired play and the word went on "to play." Mr. Leech and Mr. Myrick, ever ready for emergencies in tennis, called for gasolene, which was forthcoming speedily, and, while the Chief Executive of the United States interviewed men on the destiny of nations, the people of Washington watched nearly 200 barrels of gasolene flare up over the surface of the court. The desired result was attained and at

2 o'clock President Harding personally called play.

Singles between Williams and me opened the matches. Then Williams and Washburn decisively defeated Johnson and me, following which Williams and I nosed out Washburn and Johnson to close the program.

The second outstanding feature was the tour for the benefit of the American Committee for Devastated France. The appearance in America of Mlle. Suzanne Lenglen was due primarily to the efforts of Miss Anne Morgan, who secured the services of the famous French champion for a tour of the States, the proceeds to go to Devastated France. Mlle. Lenglen's regrettable collapse and forced departure left the Committee in a serious position. The American Tennis Association, which had coöperated with Miss Morgan in the Lenglen tour, found its clubs eager for a chance to stage matches for France but no matches available. Finally, in October, in response to the voluntary offer of several of the leading players, a team was organized that toured the East for the benefit of Devastated France. It included Mrs. Franklin I. Mallory, American champion, Miss Eleanor Goss, Miss Leslie Bancroft, Mrs. B. F. Cole, Mrs. F. H. Godfrey, Vincent Richards, Watson Washburn, N. W. Niles, R. N. Williams, W. F. Johnson and myself. Matches were staged at Orange, Short Hills, Morristown and Elizabeth, New Jersey, Green Meadow Club, Jackson Heights Club, Ardsley-on-the-Hudson,

New Rochelle, Yonkers, New York, New Haven, and Hartford, Connecticut. They proved a tremendous success financially, and France netted a sum in excess of $10,000.

PART IV: SOME SIDELIGHTS ON FAMOUS PLAYERS

PART IV: SOME SIDELIGHTS ON FAMOUS PLAYERS

INTRODUCTORY

P. T. BARNUM immortalised Lincoln's language by often quoting him with: "You can fool some of the people all of the time, and all of the people some of the time, but you can't fool all of the people all of the time." P. T. was an able judge of the public, and it is just this inability to fool all of the people all of the time that accounts for the sudden disappearance from the public eye of some one who only fooled all of the people for a little while. That person was a sham, a bluff, a gamester. He, or she, as the case may be, had no personality.

Personality needs no disguise with which to fool the people. It is not hidden in a long-hair eccentric being. That type is merely one of those who are "born every minute," as the saying goes. Personality is a dynamic, compelling force. It is a positive thing that will not be obliterated.

Personality is a sexless thing. It transcends sex. Theodore Roosevelt was a compelling personality, and his force and ability were recognized by his friends and enemies alike while the public, the masses, adored him without knowing why. Sarah Bernhardt, Eleanor Dusé, and Mary Garden carry with them a force far more potent in its appeal to the public than their mere feminine charm. They hold their public by personality. It is not trickery, but art, plus this intangible force.

The great figures in the tennis world that have held their public in their hands, all have been men of marked personality. Not all great tennis players have personality. Few of the many stars of the game can lay claim to it justly. The most powerful personality in the tennis world during my time is Norman E. Brookes, with his peculiar sphinx-like repression, mysterious, quiet, and ominous calm. Brookes repels many by his peculiar personality. He never was the popular hero that other men, notably M'Loughlin and Wilding, have been. Yet Brookes always held a gallery enthralled, not only by the sheer wizardry of his play, but by the power of his magnetic force.

Maurice E. M'Loughlin is the most remarkable example of a wonderful dynamic personality, literally carrying a public off its feet. America and England fell before the dazzling smile and vibrant force of the red-haired Californian. His whole game glittered in its radiance. His was a triumph of a popular hero.

Anthony F. Wilding, quiet, charming, and magnetic, carried his public away with him by his dynamic game. It was not the whirlwind flash of the Comet M'Loughlin that swept crowds off their feet, it was more the power of repression that compelled.

I know no other tennis players that sweep their public away with them to quite the same degree as these three men I have mentioned. R. L. Murray has much of M'Loughlin's fire, but not the spontaneity that won the hearts of the crowd. Tennis needs big personalities to give the public that glow of personal interest that helps to keep the game alive. A great personality is the property of the public. It is the price he must pay for his gift.

It is the personal equation, the star, who appeals to the public's imagination.

I do not think it is the star who keeps the game alive. It is that great class of players who play at clubs the world over, who can never rise above the dead level of mediocrity, the mass of tennis enthusiasts who play with dead racquets and old balls, and who attend all big events to witness the giants of the court, in short, "The Dubs" (with a capital D), who make tennis what it is, and to whom tennis owes its life, since they are its support and out from them have come our champions.

Champions are not born. They are made. They emerge from a long, hard school of defeat, disencouragement, and mediocrity, not because they are born tennis players, but because they are endowed with a force that transcends discouragement and cries "I will succeed."

There must be something that carries them up from the mass. It is that something which appeals in some form to the public. The public may like it, or they may dislike it, but they recognize it.

It may be personality, dogged determination, or sheer genius of tennis, for all three succeed; but be it what it may, it brings out a famous player. The quality that turns out a great player, individualizes his game so that it bears a mark peculiar to himself. I hope to be able to call to mind the outstanding qualities of some of the leading tennis players of the world.

Where to start, in a field so great, representing as it does America, the British Isles, Australia, France, Japan, South Africa, Rumania, Holland, and Greece, is not an easy task; but it is with a sense of pride and a knowledge that there is no game better fitted to end this section of my book, and no man more worthy to lead the great players of the world, that I turn to William M. Johnston, the champion of the United States of America, and my team-mate in the Davis Cup team of 1920.

CHAPTER XII

AMERICA

WILLIAM M. JOHNSTON

THE American champion is one of the really great orthodox players in the world. There is nothing eccentric, nothing freakish about his game.

Johnston is a small man, short and light; but by perfect weight-control, footwork, and timing he hits with terrific speed.

His service is a slice. Hit from the top of his reach Johnston gets power and twist on the ball with little effort. He has a wonderful forehand drive, of a top-spin variety. This shot is world famous, for never in the history of the game has so small a man hit with such terrific speed and accuracy. The racquet travels flat and then over the ball, with a peculiar wrist-snap just as the ball meets the racquet face. The shot travels deep and fast to the base-line.

Johnston's backhand is a decided "drag" or chop. He hits it with the same face of the racquet as his forehand, and with very little change in grip. It is remarkably steady and accurate, and allows Johnston to follow to the net behind it.

Johnston's volleying is hard, deep, and usually very reliable. He crouches behind his racquet and volleys directly in to the flight of the ball, hitting down. His low volleys are made with a peculiar wrist-flick that gives the rise and speed. His overhead is accurate, reliable, but not startling in its power. Johnston's game has no real weakness, while his forehand and volleying are superlative.

Johnston is a remarkable match player. He reaches his greatest game when behind. He is one of the hardest men to beat in the game owing to his utter lack of fear and the dogged determination with which he hangs on when seemingly beaten. He is quiet, modest, and a sterling sportsman. He gets a maximum result with a minimum effort.

R. N. WILLIAMS

R. N. Williams, American Champion 1914 and 1916, another of my Davis Cup team-mates, is a unique personality in the tennis world. Personally, I believe that Williams at his best is the greatest tennis player in the world, past or present. Unfortunately, that best is seldom seen, and then not for a consistent performance. He is always dangerous, and his range of variation is the greatest among any of the leading players.

Williams' service is generally a fast slice, although he at times uses an American twist. He is erratic in his delivery, scoring many aces, but piling up enormous numbers of double-faults. His ground strokes are made off the rising bound of the ball.

They are flat or slightly sliced. Never topped, but sometimes pulled. Williams' margin of safety is so small that unless his shot is perfectly hit it is useless. He hits hard at all times and makes tremendous numbers of earned points, yet his errors always exceed them, except when he strikes one of his "super" days.

His volleying is very hard, crisp, and decisive, coupled with an occasional stop volley. His use of the half volley is unequalled in modern tennis. His overhead is severe and ordinarily reliable, although he will take serious slumps overhead. He is a past master of his own style strokes, but it is an unorthodox game that should not be copied by the average player.

He is never willing to alter his game for safety's sake, and defeats himself in sheer defiance by hitting throughout a match when his strokes are not working. He is greatly praised for this unwillingness to alter his game in defeat. Personally, I think he deserves condemnation rather than praise, for it seems recklessness rather than bravery to thus seek defeat that could easily be avoided.

Williams takes tennis almost too lightly. Cheery, modest, and easy-going, he is very popular with all galleries, as his personality deserves. He is a brilliant ever-interesting light in any tennis gathering, and his game will always show sheer genius of execution even while rousing irritation by his refusal to play safe. He would rather have one super-great day and bad defeats, than no bad defeats without his day of greatness. Who shall say he is not right? We may not now agree, but Williams may yet prove to us he is right and we are wrong.

CHARLES S. GARLAND

The last member of the Davis Cup team and youngest player of the Americans is Charles S. Garland, the Yale star.

Garland is the perfect stylist, the orthodox model for ground strokes. He is an example of what stroke perfection can do.

He uses a soft slice service, of no particular peculiarity, yet places it so well that he turns it into an attack. His forehand is hit with a full swing, flat racquet face, and a slight top spin. It is deadly accurate and of moderate speed. He can put the ball at will anywhere in the court off his forehand. His backhand is slightly sliced down the line and pulled flat across the court. It is not a point winner but is an excellent defence. His overhead is steady, reliable, and accurate, but lacks aggressiveness. His high volleying is fine, deep, and fast. His low volleying is weak and uncertain. He anticipates wonderfully, and covers a tremendous amount of court. His attack is rather obvious in that he seldom plays the unusual shot, yet his accuracy is so great that he frequently beats a man who guesses his shot yet can't reach it.

N. E. Brookes stated he considered Garland one of the greatest ground-stroke players in the world.

This is true of his forehand, but his backhand lacks punch. His whole game needs speed and aggressiveness.

He is quiet, modest, and extremely popular. His perfect court manner and pleasant smile have made Garland a universal favourite in America and England. His game is the result of hard, conscientious work. There is no genius about it, and little natural talent. It is not an interesting game as it lacks brilliancy, yet it is very sound, and much better than it looks.

VINCENT RICHARDS

Vincent Richards, National Junior Champion of America and the most remarkable boy playing tennis, is a distinct personality. Richards, who is now only seventeen, won the Men's Doubles Championship of America at the age of fifteen. Richards is a born tennis player and a great tennis genius.

Richards' service is a fast slice that he follows to the net. It is speedy and very accurate. His ground strokes are both slice and drive, although the basis of his game is slice. He meets the ball on the rise and "spoons" it off his forehand. It is low, fast, but none too sure. His backhand shot is a fast twisting slice that is remarkably effective and very excellent as a defence. He is learning a flat drive.

His volleying is the great feature of his game. He is the greatest natural volleyer I have ever seen. Low and high volleying, fore- and backhand is perfect in execution. His half volleying is phenomenal.

His overhead is very severe for a boy, and carries great speed for so small a person, but it is inclined to be slightly erratic. He is tremendously fast on his feet, but it inclined to be lazy.

Vincent Richards has the greatest natural aptitude and equipment of any tennis player I have ever seen. Against it he has a temperament that is inclined to carelessness and laziness. He tends to sulkiness, which he is rapidly outgrowing. He is a delightful personality on the court, with his slight figure, tremendous speed, and merry smile. He is a second "Gus" Touchard in looks and style. I hope to see him develop to be the greatest player the world has ever seen. He gives that promise. The matter rests in Richards' hands, as his worst enemy is his temperament.

At his best he is to-day the equal of the top flight in the world. At his worst he is a child. His average is fine but not great. Travel, work, sincere effort, and a few years, should turn this astonishing boy into a marvellous player.

R. L. MURRAY

The new "California Comet," successor to M. E. M'Loughlin, is the usual sobriquet for R. L. Murray, now of Buffalo. Murray won the National Crown in 1917-1918.

His service is of the same cyclonic character as M'Loughlin. Murray is left-handed. He hits a fast cannon-ball delivery of great speed and an

American twist of extreme twist. His ground strokes
are not good, and he rushes the net at every opportunity. His forehand drive is very fast, excessively
topped, and exceedingly erratic. His backhand is a
"poke." His footwork is very poor on both shots.
He volleys very well, shooting deep to the base-line
and very accurately. His shoulder-high volleys are
marvellous. His overhead is remarkable for its
severity and accuracy. He seldom misses an overhead ball.

Murray is a terrifically hard worker, and tires
himself out very rapidly by prodigious effort. He
is a hard fighter and a hard man to beat. He works
at an enormous pace throughout the match.

He is large, spare, rangy, with dynamic energy,
and a wonderful personality that holds the gallery.
His smile is famous, while his sense of humour never
deserts him. A sportsman to his finger-tips, there
is no more popular figure in American tennis than
Murray. His is not a great game. It is a case of
a great athlete making a second-class game first
class, by sheer power of personality and fighting
ability. He is really a second M'Loughlin in his
game, his speed, and his personal charm.

WATSON WASHBURN

In contrast to Murray, Watson Washburn plays
a cool, never-hurried, never-flurried game that is
unique in American tennis.

There is little that is noteworthy of Washburn's

game. His service is a well-placed slice. His ground strokes are a peculiar "wrist-slap," almost a slice. His volleying fair, his overhead steady but not remarkable. Just a good game, well rounded but not unique. Why is Washburn great? Because, behind the big round glasses that are the main feature of Washburn on the tennis court, is a brain of the first water, directing and developing that all-round game. There is no more brilliant student of men in games than Washburn, and his persistence of attack is second only to Brookes'.

Washburn, too, is a popular player, but not in the same sense as Murray. Murray appeals to the imagination of the crowd, Washburn to its academic instincts. Washburn is a strategist, working out his match with mathematical exactness, and always checking up his men as he goes along.

There is no tennis player whose psychology I admire more than Washburn's. He is never beaten until the last point is played, and he is always dangerous, no matter how great a lead you hold over him.

Another case of the second-class game being made first class, but this time it is done by mental brilliancy.

WALLACE F. JOHNSON

Here is another case of a second-class game being used in a first-class manner, getting first-class results through the direction of a first-class tennis brain. Johnson is not the brilliant, analytical mind of

Washburn, but for pure tennis genius Johnson ranks nearly the equal of Brookes.

Johnson is a one-stroke player. He uses a peculiar slice shot hit from the wrist. He uses it in service, ground strokes, volleying, and lobbing. It is a true one-stroke game, yet by sheer audacity of enterprise and wonderful speed of foot Wallace Johnson has for years been one of the leading players of America.

SAMUEL HARDY

The overwhelming success of the American Davis Cup team in 1920, when we brought back the cup from Australia was due in no small measure to the wonderful generalship displayed by one man, our Captain Samuel Hardy.

The hardest part of any such trip is the attention to training, relaxation and accommodations for the team and only perfect judgment can give the comfort so needed by a team. It is to Captain Hardy that the team owes its perfect condition throughout the entire 3,000 miles we journeyed after the cup. Yet Captain Hardy's success was far bigger than that, for by his tact, charming personality and splendid sportsmanship at all times he won a place for us in the hearts of every country we visited. Hardy, although a non-playing member of the team, is a great tennis player. He is one of the best doubles players America has produced. His clever generalship and wonderful knowledge of the game proved of inestimable value to the team in laying out our plan of attack in the Davis Cup matches themselves.

Clever, charming, just and always full of the most delightful humour, Hardy was an ideal Captain who kept his team in the best of spirits no matter how badly we might have been playing or how depressing appeared our outlook.

CARL FISCHER

I am including in my analysis of players a boy who is just gaining recognition but who I believe is to be one of the great stars of the future, Carl Fischer of Philadelphia.

Young Fischer, who is only 19, is a brilliant, hard hitting left-hander. He has already won the Eastern Pennsylvania Championship, been runner-up to Wallace Johnson in the Pennsylvania State, Philadelphia Championship and Middle States event, besides holding the Junior Championship of Pennsylvania for two years. He won the University of Pennsylvania Championship in his freshman year.

His service is a flat delivery of good speed, at times, verging on the American twist. His ground game carries top spin drives forehand and backhand. His volleying and overhead are severe and powerful but prone to be erratic. Fischer is an all court player of the most modern type. He is aggressive, almost too much so at times as he wastes a great deal of energy by useless rushing. He needs steadiness and a willingness to await his opening but gives promise of rounding into a first class player, as his stroke equipment is second to none.

MARSHALL ALLEN

Far out in the Pacific Northwest in Seattle, Washington, is a young player who bids fair to some day be world famous. It is quite possible he may never arrive at all.

Marshall Allen is a typical Western player. Allen has a hurricane service that is none too reliable. His forehand drive is reminiscent of McLoughlin. It is a furious murderous attack when it goes in and quite useless when it is off. Allen's backhand is a flat drive played to either side with equal ease. At present it is erratic but shows great promise. Allen volleys at times brilliantly, but is uncertain and at times misses unaccountably. His overhead is remarkably brilliant and severe, but also erratic. He reaches great heights and sinks to awful depths. If Marshall Allen consolidates his game and refines the material he has at hand he should be a marvellous player. If he allows his love of speed to run away with his judgment at the expense of accuracy and steadiness he will never rise above the second class. Time will tell the story. I look to see him world famous.

OUR RISING JUNIORS

For a moment I am going to pay tribute to some boys who I look to see among the stars of the future.

They are all juniors less than eighteen at the time of writing.

First in importance comes Arnold W. Jones, of Providence, R. I., who accompanied me to France and England in 1921, where he made a fine record. Young Jones has a splendid all-court game, with a remarkable forehand drive but a tendency to weariness in his backhand and service. His volleying is excellent. His overhead erratic.

Second to Jones I place Charles Watson III of Philadelphia. Here is a boy with a most remarkable resemblance to Chuck Garland in style of his game. Watson has a fine service, beautiful ground strokes fore and backhand and a more aggressive volley than Garland. His overhead lacks punch. He is the cleverest court general among the juniors.

Phillip Bettens of San Francisco is a possible successor to Billy Johnston. Bettens has a terrific forehand drive and a rushing net attack. He needs to steady up his game, but he is a player of great promise.

Armand Marion of Seattle, Washington, is another boy with a finely rounded game who, given experience and seasoning, bids fair to become a great star. Marion does not have enough punch yet and needs to gain decisiveness of attack.

Charles Wood of New York, W. W. Ingraham of Providence, Milo Miller and Eric Wood of Philadelphia, John Howard of Baltimore, and others are of equal class and of nearly equal promise to the boys I have mentioned.

In the younger class of boys those under 15, one finds many youngsters already forming real style. The boy who shows the greatest promise and today the best all-round game, equalling in potential power even Vincent Richards at the same age, is Alexander L. (Sandy) Wiener of Philadelphia. At fourteen young Weiner is a stylist of the highest all-court type.

Among the other boys who may well develop into stars in the future are Meredith W. Jones, Arthur Ingraham, Jr., Andrew Clarke Ingraham, Miles Valentine, Raymond Owen, Richard Chase, Neil Sullivan, Henry Neer, and Edward Murphy.

There are many other great players I would like to analyse, but space forbids. Among our leaders are Roland Roberts, John Strachan, C. J. Griffin, Davis, and Robert Kinsey in California; Walter T. Hayes, Ralph Burdock, and Heath Byford in the Middle West; Howard Voshell, Harold Throckmorton, Conrad B. Doyle, Craig Biddle, Richard Harte, Colket Caner, Nathaniel W. Niles, H. C. Johnson, Dean Mathey, and many others of equal fame in the East.

CHAPTER XIII

BRITISH ISLES

J. C. PARKE

THERE is no name in tennis history of the past decade more famous than that of J. C. Parke. In twelve months, during 1912 and 1913, he defeated Brookes, Wilding, and M'Loughlin—a notable record; and now in 1920, after his wonderful work in the World War, he returns to tennis and scores a decisive victory over W. M. Johnston.

Parke is essentially a base-line player. His service is soft, flat, but well placed. His ground strokes are hit with an almost flat racquet face and a peculiar short swing. He uses a pronounced snap of the wrist. He slices his straight backhand shot, but pulls his drive 'cross court. It is Parke's famous running drive down the line that is the outstanding feature of his game. Parke was a ten-second hundred-yard man in college, and still retains his remarkable speed of foot. He hits his drive while running at top speed and translates his weight to the ball. It shoots low and fast down the line. It is a marvellous stroke.

Parke's volleying is steady and well placed but not decisive. His overhead is reliable and accurate,

but lacks "punch." The great factor of Parke's
game is his uncanny ability to produce his greatest
game under the greatest stress. I consider him one
of the finest match players in the world. His tacti-
cal knowledge and brainy attack are all the more
dangerous, because he has phenomenal power of
defence and fighting qualities of the highest order.
There is no finer sportsman in tennis than Parke.
Generous, quiet, and modest, Parke is deservedly a
popular figure with the tennis world.

A. R. F. KINGSCOTE

The most recent star to reach the heights of fame
in English tennis is Major A. R. F. Kingscote.
Kingscote has played good tennis for some years;
but it was only in 1919, following his excellent work
in the War, that he showed his true worth. He
defeated Gobert in sequence sets in the Davis Cup
tie at Deauville, and followed by defeating Anderson
in Australia and carrying Patterson to a hard match.
Since then he has steadily improved and this season
found him the leading figure of the British team.

Kingscote played much of his early tennis with
R. N. Williams in Switzerland during 1910 and
1911. The effect of this training is easily seen on
his game to-day for, without Williams' dash and extreme brilliancy, their strokes are excuted in very
much the same style.

Kingscote's service is a fast slice, well placed and
cleverly disguised. It carries a great deal of pace

and twist. His ground strokes are hit off the rising
bound of the ball, with a flat raquet face or a slight
slice. His wonderful speed of foot offsets his lack
of height, and he hits either side with equal facility.
There are no gaps in Kingscote's game. It is perfectly rounded. His favourite forehand shot is
'cross court, yet he can hit equally well down the
line. His backhand is steady, very accurate and
deceptive, but rather lacks speed. His volleying
is remarkable for his court covering and angles, but
is not the decisive win of Williams or Johnston. He
is the best volleyer in the British Isles. His overhead is realiable and accurate for so short a man, but
at times is prone to lack speed.

Kingscote is a sound tactician without the stra-
tegic brilliance of Parke. He is a fine match player
and dogged fighter. Witness his 5-set battle with
me in the Championships, after being match point
down in the fourth set, and his 5-set struggle with
Johnston in the Davis Cup. It is a slight lack of
decisiveness all round that keeps Kingscote just a
shade below the first flight. He is a very fine player,
who may easily become a top-notch man. His pleasant, modest manner and generous sportsmanship
make him an ideal opponent, and endear him to the
gallery.

H. ROPER BARRETT

One of the real tennis tacticians, a man who is
to-day a veteran of many a notable encounter, yet
still dangerous at all times, is H. Roper Barrett.

A member of every Davis Cup team since the matches were inaugurated, a doubles player of the highest strategy, Roper Barrett needs no introduction or analysis. His game is soft. His service looks a joke. In reality it is hard to hit, for Barrett pushes it to the most unexpected places. His ground strokes, soft, short, and low, are ideal doubles shots. He angles off the ball with a short shove in the direction. He can drive hard when pressed, but prefers to use the slow poke.

His volleying is the acme of finesse. He angles soft to the side-lines, stop volleys the hardest drives successfully. He picks openings with an unerring eye. His overhead lacks "punch," but is steady and reliable.

Barrett is a clever mixer of shots. He is playing the unexpected shot to the unexpected place. His sense of anticipation is remarkable, and he retrieves the most unusual shots. It is his great tennis tactics that make him noteworthy. His game is round but not wonderful.

THE LOWES, A. H. AND F. G.

The famous brothers, called indiscriminately the Lowes, are two of the best base-line players in the British Isles. Both men play almost identical styles, and at a distance are very hard to tell apart.

Gordon Lowe uses a slice service, while Arthur serves with a reverse spin. Neither man has a dangerous delivery. Both are adequate and hard to win earned points from.

The ground strokes of the Lowes are very orthodox. Full swing, top spin drives fore- and backhand, straight or 'cross court, are hit with equal
facility. The Lowes volley defensively and only
come in to the let when pulled in by a short shot.
Their overhead work is average.

Their games are not startling. There is nothing
to require much comment. Both men are excellent
tennis players of the true English school: fine base-
line drivers, but subject to defeat by any aggressive
volleyer. It is a lack of aggressiveness that holds
both men down, for they are excellent court coverers,
fine racquet wielders, but do not rise to real heights.
The Lowes could easily defeat any player who was
slightly off his game, as they are very steady and
make few mistakes. Neither would defeat a first-
class player at his best.

T. M. MAVROGORDATO

One of the most consistent winners in English tennis for a span of years is a little man with a big
name, who is universally and popularly known as
"Mavro."

"Mavro" added another notable victory in 1920,
when he defeated R. N. Williams in the last eight
in the World Championships. "Mavro" has always
been a fine player, but he has never quite scaled the
top flight.

His game is steadiness personified. He shoves his
service in the court at the end of a prodigious swing

that ends in a poke. It goes where he wishes it.
His ground strokes are fine, in splendid form, very
accurate and remarkably fast for so little effort.
Mavro is not large enough to hit hard, but owing
to his remarkable footwork he covers a very large
territory in a remarkably short space of time. His
racquet work is a delight to a student of orthodox
form. His volleying is accurate, steady, well placed
but defensive. He has no speed or punch to his
volley. His overhead is steady to the point of being
unique. He is so small that it seems as if anyone
could lob over his head, but his speed of foot is so
great that he invariably gets his racquet on it and
puts it back deep.

Mavro turns defence into attack by putting the
ball back in play so often that his opponent gets
tired hitting it and takes unnecessary chances. His
accuracy is so great that it makes up for his lack
of speed. His judgment is sound but not brilliant.
He is a hard-working, conscientious player who deserves his success.

There are many other players who are interesting
studies. The two Australians, now living in England, and to all intents and purposes Englishmen,
Randolph Lycett and F. M. B. Fisher, are distinct
and interesting types of players. C. P. Dixon,
Stanley Doust, M. J. G. Ritchie, Max Woosnam,
the rising young star, P. M. Davson, A. E. Beamish,
W. C. Crawley, and scores of other excellent players, will carry the burden of English tennis success-

fully for some years. Yet new blood must be found to infuse energy into the game. Speed is a necessity in English tennis if the modern game is to reach its greatst height in the British Isles.

Youth must be seen soon, if the game in the next ten years is to be kept at its present level. Parke, Mavro, Ritchie, Dixon, Barrett, etc., cannot go on for ever, and young players must be developed to take their places. The coming decade is the crucial period of English tennis. I hope and believe it will be successfully passed.

A. R. F. KINGSCOTE
British Isles

J. C. PARKE
British Isles

GERALD PATTERSON
Australia

T. M. MAVROGORDATO
British Isles

LOUIS RAYMOND
South Africa

B. I. C. NORTON
South Africa

Z. F. SHIMIDZU
Japan

N. MISHU
Roumania

CHAPTER XIV

FRANCE AND JAPAN

France

ANDRÉ GOBERT

ONE of the most picturesque figures and delightfully polished tennis games in the world are joined in that volatile, temperamental player, André Gobert of France. He is a typically French product, full of finesse, art, and nerve, surrounded by the romance of a wonderful war record of his people in which he bore a magnificent part, yet unstable, erratic, and uncertain. At his best he is invincible. He is the great master of tennis. At his worst he is mediocre. Gobert is at once a delight and a disappointment to a student of tennis.

Gobert's service is marvellous. It is one of the great deliveries of the world. His great height (he is 6 feet 4 inches) and tremendous reach enable him to hit a flat delivery at frightful speed, and still stand an excellent chance of it going in court. He uses very little twist, so the pace is remarkably fast. Yet Gobert lacks confidence in his service. If his opponent handles it successfully

Gobert is apt to slow it up and hit it soft, thus throwing away one of the greatest assets.

His ground strokes are hit in beautiful form. Gobert is the exponent of the most perfect form in the world to-day. His swing is the acme of beauty. The whole stroke is perfection. He hits with a flat, slightly topped drive, feet in excellent position, and weight well controlled. It is uniform, backhand and forehand. His volleying is astonishing. He can volley hard or soft, deep or short, straight or angled with equal ease, while his tremendous reach makes him nearly impossible to pass at the net. His overhead is deadly, fast, and accurate, and he kills a lob from anywhere in the court.

Why is not Gobert the greatest tennis player in the world? Personally I believe it is lack of confidence, a lack of fighting ability when the breaks are against him, and defeat may be his due. It is a peculiar thing in Gobert, for no man is braver than he, as his heroism during the War proved. It is simply lack of tennis confidence. It is an over-abundance of temperament. In victory Gobert is invincible, in defeat he is apt to be almost mediocre.

Gobert is delightful personally. His quick wit and sense of humour always please the tennis public. His courteous manner and genial sportsmanship make him universally popular. His stroke equipment is unsurpassed in the tennis world.

I unqualifiedly state that I consider him the most perfect tennis player, as regards strokes and footwork, in the world to-day; but he is not the greatest player. Victory is the criterion of a match player, and Gobert has not proved himself a great victor.

Gobert is probably the finest indoor player in the world, while he is very great on hard courts; but his grass play is not the equal of many others. I heartily recommend Gobert's style to all students of the game, and endorse him as a model for strokes.

W. LAURENTZ

Another brilliant, erratic and intensely interesting figure that France has given the tennis world is Laurentz, the wonderful young player, who at the age of seventeen defeated A. F. Wilding.

Laurentz is a cyclonic hitter of remarkable speed and brilliance, but prone to very severe lapses. His service is of several varieties, all well played. He uses an American twist as his regular delivery, but varies it with a sharp slice, a reverse twist of great spin, and a fast cannon-ball smash. Laurentz is very versatile. He has excellent orthodox drives, fore- and backhand, and a competent forehand chop.

His volleying is brilliant almost beyond description, but very erratic. He is very fast on his feet, and anticipates remarkably well. He will make the most hair-raising volleys, only to fall down inexplicably the next moment on an easy shot. His overhead is like his volley, severe, brilliant, but uncertain.

Laurentz is a very hard worker, and, unlike Gobert, is always at his best when behind. He is a fair fighter and a great match player. His defeats are due more to over-anxiety than to lack of fight.

He is temperamental, sensational, and brilliant, a sportsman of the highest type, quick to recognize his opponent's good work and to give full credit for it. He is one of the most interesting players now before the public.

He is a clever court general but not a great tennis thinker, playing more by instinct than by a really deep-laid plan of campaign. Laurentz might beat anyone in the world on his day or lose to the veriest dub when at his worst.*

J. SAMAZIEUHL

The New French Champion of 1921 who defeated André Gobert most unexpectedly in the challenge round, is an interesting player of the mental type. He is anything but French in his game. His style is rather that of the crafty American or English player than the hard-hitting Frenchman.

Samazieuhl is an exponent of crafty patball. His service is a medium pace slice, well placed but not decisive. His ground strokes are a peculiar stiff arm chop varied at times with an equally cramped drive, yet his extreme mobility allows him to cover a tremendous amount of court, while his return, which is well disguised, is capable of great angles. His volleying is reliable but lacks severity and punch. He makes excellent low volleys, but cannot put away shoulder high balls while his overhead is not deadly.

It is Samazieuhl's clever generalship and his abil-

* It was with deepest regret the news of his death reached us, as this edition went to press.

ity to recover seemingly impossible shots that win matches for him. He is a comparatively new tournament player, and should improve greatly as he gains confidence and experience.

R. DANET

One of the most interesting young players in France is R. Danet, who has come to the fore in the past few years. This boy, for he is little more, has a hard hitting brilliant game of great promise.

His service is a speedy slice. He drives with great speed, if as yet with none too much accuracy, off both fore and backhand. His net attack is very severe while overhead he is deadly. His speed of foot is remarkable, and he is a very hard worker. His limitations are in his lack of a set plan of attack and the steady adherence to any given method of play. He throws away too many easy chances, but this will correct itself as time goes on and Danet has fought through more tournaments. I consider him a player of great promise.

Max Decugis and Brugnon, the two remaining members of the 1920 Davis Cup team of France, present totally different types. Decugis, crafty, cool, and experienced, is the veteran of many long seasons of match play. He is a master tactician, and wins most of his matches by outgeneralling the other player. Burgnon is brilliant, flashy, hard hitting, erratic, and inexperienced. He is very young, hardly twenty years of age. He has a fine fore-hitting style and excellent net attack, but lacks confidence and a certain knowledge of tennis fundamentals. A few years' experience will do wonders for him.

The French style of play commends itself to me very highly. I enjoy watching the well-executed strokes, beautiful mobile footwork of these dashing players. It is more a lack of dogged determination to win, than in any stroke fault that one finds the reason for French defeats. The temperamental genius of this great people carries with it a lack of stability that can be the only explanation for the sudden crushing and unexpected defeats their representatives receive on the tennis courts.

I was particularly impressed during my visit to France by the large numbers of children playing tennis and the style of game displayed. The sport shows a healthy increase and should produce some fine players within the next ten years.

Keen competition is the corrective measure for temperamental instability and with the advent of many new players in French tennis I would not be surprised to see a marked decrease of unexpected defeats of their leading players.

Japan

A new element has entered the tennis world in the last decade. The Orient has thrust its shadow over the courts in the persons of a small group of remarkable tennis players, particularly Ichija

Kumagae and Zenzo Shimidzu, the famous Japanese stars.

Kumagae, who for some years reigned supreme in Japan and Honolulu, has lived in America for the past three years. Shimidzu is a product of Calcutta, where he has lived for some years.

No player has caused more discussion than Kumagae, unless it is Shimidzu; while surely no man received more critical comment than Shimidzu, except Kumagae. The press of America and England have vied with each other in exploiting these two men. There was unanimity of opinion concerning these two men in one respect. No finer sportsmen nor more delightful opponents can be found than these Japanese. They have won the respect and friendship of all who have met them.

Kumagae is the speedier tennis player. He came to America in 1916, the possessor of a wonderful forehand drive and nothing else. Kumagae is left-handed, which made his peculiar shots all the harder to handle. He met with fair success during the year; his crowning triumph was his defeat of W. M. Johnston at Newport in five sets. He lost to J. J. Armstrong, Watson M. Washburn, and George M. Church. He learned much during his year in America, and returned to Japan a wiser man, with a firm determination to add to his tennis equipment.

In 1917 Kumagae returned to America to enter business in New York. Once established there he began developing his game. First he learned an American twist service and then strengthened his backhand. That year he suffered defeat at the hands of Walter T. Hayes and myself. He was steadily improving. He now started coming to the net and learning to volley. He is not yet a good low volleyer, and never will be while he uses the peculiar grip common to his people; but his high volleying and overhead are now excellent. Last year Kumagae reached his top form and was ranked third in America. His defeats were by Johnston, Vincent Richards, and myself; while he defeated Murray, S. H. Voshell, Vincent Richards, and me, as well as countless players of less note.

The season of 1920 found Kumagae sweeping all before him, since Johnston, Williams, Garland, and I were away on the Davis Cup trip. Williams barely defeated him in a bitter match, just previously to sailing. Kumagae left America in the middle of the summer to compete in the Olympic games, representing Japan.

Kumagae is still essentially a base-line player of marvellous accuracy of shot and speed of foot. His drive is a lethal weapon that spreads destruction among his opponents. His backhand is a severe "poke," none too accurate, but very deadly when it goes in. His service overhead and high volley are all severe and reliable. His low volley is the weak spot in an otherwise great game. Kumagae cannot handle a chop, and dislikes grass-court play, as the ball bounds too low for his peculiar "loop" drive. He is one of the greatest hard-court players in the world, and one of the most dangerous opponents at any time on any surface.

Shimidzu is to-day as dangerous as Kumagae. He, too, is a base-line player, but lacks Kumagae's terrific forehand drive. Shimidzu has a superior backhand to Kumagae, but his weak service rather offsets this. His low volleying is far superior to Kumagae, while his high volleying and overhead are quite his equal. He has all the fighting qualities in his game that make Kumagae so dangerous, but he has not had the experience. Shimidzu learns very quickly, and I look to see him a great factor in the game in future years.

Both Shimidzu and Kumagae are marvellous court coverers, and seem absolutely untiring. They are "getters" of almost unbelievable activity, and accurate to a point that seems uncanny. Both men hit to the lines with a certainty that makes it very dangerous to attempt to take the net on anything except a deep forcing shot that hurries them.

With such players as Kumagae and Shimidzu, followed by S. Kashio and K. Yamasaki, and the late H. Mikami, Japan is a big factor in future tennis. 1922 will again see Japan challenging for the Davis Cup, and none but a first-class team can stop them. The advent of a Japanese team with such players will mean that this year we must call out our best to repel the Oriental invasion: so competition receives another stimulus that should raise our standard of play.

The probability of journeying to Japan to challenge for the Davis Cup is not so remote but that we must consider it as a future possibility.

CHAPTER XV

SPAIN AND THE CONTINENT

Spain

A NEW factor entered the arena of world tennis in 1921 in the appearance of a Spanish Davis Cup team. Among their number is a star who bids fair to become one of the greatest players the world has ever seen. A scintillating personality, brilliant versatile game, and fighting temperament placed this young unknown in the first rank in one year of competition.

MANUEL ALONZO

Seldom have I seen such wonderful natural abilities as are found in this young Spaniard. Here is a player par excellence if he develops as he gives promise. Alonzo is young, about 25, slight, attractive in personality and court manners, quick to the point of almost miraculous court covering. He is a great attraction at any tournament.

His service is a fairly fast American twist. It is not remarkable but is at least more severe than the average continental delivery.

Alonzo has a terrific forehand drive that is the closest rival to W. M. Johnston's of any shot I have seen. He is reliable on this stroke, either straight or cross-court from the deep court but if drawn in to mid-court is apt to miss it. His backhand is a flat drive, accurate and low but rather slow and in the main defensive.

His volleying is at once a joy and a disappointment. Such marvellous angles and stop volleys off difficult drives! Yet immediately on top of a dazzling display Alonzo will throw away the easiest sort of a high volley by a pitiable fluke.

His overhead is at once severe, deadly and reliable. He smashes with speed and direction. It is not only in his varied stroke equipment that Alonzo is great but in his marvellous footwork. Such speed of foot and lightning turning I have never before seen on a tennis court. He is a quicker man than Norman E. Brookes and higher praise I cannot give. I look to see Alonzo, who today loses matches through lack of resource, become by virtue of experience and tournament play the greatest player on the continent.

His brother, J. M. Alonzo, although nowhere in Manuel's class, is a fine all court player as are Count de Gomar and Flaquer, the remaining members of the Cup team. If Alonzo and his teammates are an indication of the type of players Spain is developing a new and powerful factor in the tennis world is entering the field to stay.

Some Other Champions

There are some individual players of interest from the countries where tennis as a game has not reached a place worthy of national analysation but who deserve mention among the great players of the world.

First among them comes Nicholas Mishu of Rumania.

N. MISHU

What can I say of Mishu? As a tennis player he defies analysis. His game is a freak. He adores to do the unusual and his game abounds in freak shots that Mishu executes with remarkable skill. He has many and varied services, underhand cuts, fore and backhand, a "push" off his nose, and even one serve where he turns his back on the court and serves the ball back over his head.

His drives are cramped in swing and hit with excessive top spin. His footwork is a defiance of all rules. His volleying game looks like an accident, yet Mishu produces results. In 1921 he beat A. H. Gobert in the World's Hard Court Championship at St. Cloud. Mishu is a winner. I don't know how he does it but he does. He is above all a unique personality. Cheery, individual, at times eccentric, Mishu is a popular figure in tournaments abroad. He plays with a verve and abandon that appeals to the European galleries while his droll humour and good nature make him a delightful opponent.

J. WASHER

Belgium is represented by J. Washer, my opponent in the final round of the Hard Court Championship of the World in 1921. Washer is a fine orthodox tennis player. His service is a well placed twist delivery of medium pace. He has a terrific forehand drive that gains in effectiveness owing to the fact he is a left-hander. Like so many players with a pronounced strength, he covers up an equally pronounced weakness by using the strength. Washer has a very feeble backhand for so fine a player. He pokes his backhand when he is unable to run around it.

His overhead is strong, speedy and reliable. His volleying lacks punch and steadiness. He has had little tournament experience and shows promise of great improvement if given the opportunity.

E. TEGNER

Denmark is represented by a player of promise and skill in the person of E. Tegner. This young star defeated W. H. Laurentz at St. Cloud in the Hard Court Championship of the World in 1921 when the latter was holder of the title.

Tegner is a baseling player of fine style. His strokes are long free drives of fine pace and depth. His service is hardly adequate for first flight tennis, yet while his ground game cannot make up for the lack of aggression in his net attack. Tegner is not of championship quality at the moment but his youth allows him plenty of time to acquire that tournament experience needed to fill in the gaps in his game. He is a cool, clever court general and should develop rapidly within the next few years.

H. L. DE MORPURGO

The Italian champion, H. L. de Morpurgo, is a product of his own country and England where he attended college. He is a big, rangy man of great strength. He uses a terrific service of great speed but little control on his first ball and an exaggerated American twist on the second of such extreme contortion that even his great frame wears down under it.

His ground game is of flat drives that lack sufficient pace and accuracy to allow him to reap the full benefit of his really excellent net attack. His volleying is very good owing to his great reach. His overhead, like his service, is hard but erratic. Unfortunately he is slow on his feet and thus loses much of the advantage of his large reach. He seems to lack confidence in his game but that should come with more experience.

A. ZERLENDI

Tennis in Greece. No! not in ancient times but in modern, for that little country has a remarkable little baseline star, by name A. Zerlendi. This man is a baseliner of the most pronounced type. He gets everything he can put his racquet to. He reminds me irresistibly of Mavrogordato, seemingly reaching nothing yet they all come back. I cannot adequately analyse his game because his first principle is to put back the ball no matter how, and this he carries into excellent effect. Zerlendi is a match winner first and a stylist second.

CHAPTER XVI

THE COLONIES

Australasia

THE death of that sterling sportsman, Anthony F. Wilding, and the natural decline in the playing powers of Norman E. Brookes, owing to the advance of years and his war experiences, leave Australasia (Australia and New Zealand) in a somewhat uncertain condition regarding its tennis prospects.

NORMAN E. BROOKES

Volumes have been written about N. E. Brookes and his tennis genius, but I would not feel right if I could not pay at least a slight tribute to the greatest tennis player and genius of all time.

There is no need to dwell on Brookes' shots, his marvellous mechanical perfection, his peculiar volleying style, his uncanny anticipation. All these are too well known to need my feeble description. They are but the expression of that wonderful brain and dominant personality that lie behind that sphinx-like face we know as Brookes'.

To see across the net those ever-restless, ever-that is very severe and consistent, but his backhand . . . Where in all the rest of tennis history was there a first-class man with a backhand so fundamentally wrong? His grip is bad, he pulls up on the ball and "loops" it high in the air. I do not mean Patterson always misses his backhand. He does not. He even makes remarkable shots off it at times, but, if Patterson is pressed, his backhand is the first portion of his game to crack, because it is hit inherently wrong.

Patterson relies mainly on speed to win matches. He is not a strategist, and finesse is not part of his tennis equipment. He has a magnificent physique, and relies largely on his strength to carry him through a long match and win in the end.

He is very quiet, and inclined to be somewhat careless on the court, unless pressed, when his businesslike, determined play shows what a great match player Patterson can become. He produces his best game at the crucial moment of the match. Patterson is a superior match player to his real tennis ability. His is not truly a top-notch game. It has superlative features, but its whole texture is not of the finest.

Patterson owes much of his success in 1919 to Brookes, under whose guidance he played. The absence of the master mind directing his attack proved a decided handicap in 1920, and Patterson's attack was not so certain nor sustained as in the previous season. Patterson's game plus Brookes' strategy would be a great combination in one man.

moving eyes, picking the openings in my never too-well guarded court, and know that against me is pitted the greatest tennis brain of the century, is to call upon me to produce my best. That is what my match with Brookes meant to me, and still does to-day. Brookes should be an inspiration to every tennis player, for he has proved the power of mind over matter in tennis: "Age cannot wither nor custom stale his infinite variety."

Brookes is the most eminently just man on a tennis court I have ever met, for no excitement or emotion clouds his eyesight or judgment in de-cisions. He cannot abide bad decisions, yet he hates them quite as much when they favour him as when they are against him. I admit frankly I am a great admirer of Brookes, personally and from every tennis sense. He is a master that I as a student of the game feel proud to study under.

GERALD PATTERSON

Australia's leading player, Gerald Patterson, is one of the most remarkable combinations of tennis virtues and tennis faults I have ever seen.

Patterson has a wonderful service. He has speed, direction, control, and all kinds of twist. He hits his service consistently hard and puts it in. His overhead is the most remarkable in the game. He can kill from any place in the court. His shot is clean, with little effort, yet carries terrific speed. His volleying above the net is almost faultless on his forehand. He has an excellent forehand drive

PAT O'HARA WOOD

This young Australian is one of the greatest doubles players in the world and bids fair to press the leading singles stars close.

Pat O'Hara Wood is a player without a weakness, yet also one without a strength. He is a typical all court player with no outstanding feature to his game unless it be his volleying. Pat Wood has a natural aptitude for doubles which at times seriously interferes with his singles game.

His service is a well placed speedy slice that he mixes up well. It is not a great delivery but very effective. His ground strokes, taken on the rising bounces, are flat drives, accurate and varied as to direction but lacking punch. He does not hit hard enough. He is a brilliant volleyer, cutting off at sharp angles the hardest drives. His overhead is erratic. At times he is deadly overhead but is prone to lapses into uncertainty. He is remarkably quick and speedy of foot. His sense of anticipation is magnificent. His generalship good, though not brilliant. It is lack of punch, the inability to put the ball away, that keeps Pat O'Hara Wood from the first flight in singles.

Clever, blessed with a keen sense of humour, a sterling sportsman and delightful opponent, Pat O'Hara Wood is a big asset to tennis and a man who is needed in the game.

J. C. HAWKES

The youngest of the Australasian players and a boy of great promise is Jack Hawkes. He is only 22 and young in the game for his age.

Let me state now I do not approve of Hawkes' style. His footwork is wrong, hopelessly wrong and I fear that unless he corrects it, it may keep him from attaining the place his natural abilities promise. "Austral," the famous critic, describes him as "having the genius of the game."

Jack Hawkes has an exaggerated American twist service that, since he is a left-hander, places an unnecessary strain on his heart muscles. It carries terrific twist but little speed and does not pay him for the amount of energy he expends.

His forehand drive is excellent, fast, deep, and well placed, yet in making this he steps away from the ball, again wasting energy. His backhand is a poke and very unreliable. To save it he runs around everything possible, again causing unnecessary exertion. His volleying is brilliant while his overhead is magnificent.

Hawkes' waste of energy has cost him many a match, yet for all the inherent defects in his game he is so clever in using what he has, his tactics are so good for so young a player that I believe he will be one of the leading players of the world in a few years. Under the watchful eyes of Norman Brookes I foresee Hawkes changing his footwork to at least a reasonable copy of the old master.

J. O. ANDERSON

This young player is again a promise rather than a star. He is a big, rangy, hard-hitting type like Gerald Patterson. He is crude, at times careless and unfortunately handicapped in 1920 and 1921 by a severe illness that only allowed him to resume play in the middle of the latter year. His ground strokes are flat drives fore and backhand. His forehand is a particularly fine shot. He hits it with a short sharp snap of his arm that imparts great speed and yet hides the direction. His backhand is defensive. His volleying clever, accurate but soft. His overhand severe and reliable. His service flat, fast and dangerous.

He needs finesse, experience and season, with which he may well become one of the greatest players as the fundamental potentialities are there.

NORMAN PEACH

The steady base-line game of England has its exponent in Australia in Norman Peach. He has a beautiful driving game, with adequate but not severe service, that one finds so much in England. At times Peach will advance to the net but his volleying and overhead are secondary to his base-line game. He is not a great tennis player but is certainly one of high standard of play. He is just below the first flight in Australia.

R. V. Thomas is one of the finest doubles players

in the world as is amply attested by his win of the world's title in 1919 with Pat O'Hara Wood and their two successive wins of the Australian Championship in 1919-20. Thomas with his hard-hitting off the ground, and his brilliant volleying is a fine foil for Pat Wood's steady accuracy.

Just a word about one veteran, a good friend of mine, who is again playing fine tennis, Rodney L. Heath, hero of the famous Davis Cup match in 1911 when he defeated W. A. Larned, is again in the game.

Heath with his long beautiful groundstrokes, forehand, or backhand, his incisive crisp volleys and fine generalship based on young experience, is a notable figure in the tennis world.

The mantle of Wilding and Brookes must fall on the shoulders of a really great player. Who it will be is hard to say at present. No outstanding figure looms on the horizon at the time of writing.

South Africa

The 1920 South African Davis Cup team players, following their disastrous defeat by Holland, journeyed to England for the Championship and following tournaments, and I had the opportunity of studying three players of great promise. The remaining two were excellent, but hardly as exceptional as the former.

Charles Winslow, the leading player in the team, has a remarkable versatile game. He uses a high, bounding service of good speed, which at times he follows to the net. His best ground stroke is a severe chop, not unlike Wallace F. Johnson. He has a good drive both forehand and backhand, which he only uses when pressed or in attempting to pass a net man. He volleys very well, and covers the net quickly. His overhead is very severe, steady, and reliable. He is a fine natural player just below the top flight. He is an excellent strategist, and mixes his shots very well. He has exceptionally fast footwork, and repeatedly runs around his backhand to chop diagonally across the court in a manner very similar to Johnson.

B. I. C. Norton, the South African champion, a youngster of twenty, is a phenomenal player of extreme brilliancy. He has everything in stroke equipment, drives, slices, volleys, and a fine service and overhead. Unfortunately Norton regards his tennis largely as a joke. His judgment is therefore faulty, and he is apt to loaf on the court. He tries the most impossible shots that sometimes go in; and in the main, his court generalship is none too good.

He is an irrepressible boy, and his merry smile and chatter make him a tremendous favourite with the gallery. He has a very strong personality that should carry him a long way.

Louis Raymond, the left-handed star of the South Africans, has an excellent ground game coupled with a good service and fair volleying and overhead. His game is not remarkable. He is a hard-working, deserving player who attains success by industry

rather than natural talent.   His judgment is sound
and methods of play orthodox, except for a tendency
to run around his backhand.

C. R. Blackbeard, the youngest member of the
team, and G. H. Dodd, its captain, are both very
excellent players of the second flight.   Blackbeard
is very young, not yet twenty, and may develop
into a star.   At present he chops too much, and is
very erratic.

.   .   .   .

There are many other players whom I would
analyse if I had the time or space; but in these days
of paper shortage and ink scarcity, conservation is
the keynote of the times.

Let me turn for a few moments to the women
whose fame in the tennis world is the equal of the
men I have been analysing.

CHAPTER XVII

FAMOUS WOMEN PLAYERS

Women's Tennis

THE great boom that featured the whole tennis season of 1921 in America found one of its most remarkable manifestations in the increased amount of play, higher standard of competition and remarkable growth of public interest in women's tennis.

England has led, and still leads, the world in women's tennis. The general standard of play is on a higher scale and there is more tournament play in England than elsewhere. France, with Mlle. Suzanne Lenglen, Mme. Billout (Mlle. Brocadies) and Mme. Golding, forces England closely for European supremacy, but until recent years America, except for individuals, has been unable to reach the standard of women's tennis found abroad.

Miss May Sutton, now Mrs. Thomas H. Bundy, placed American colours in the field by her wonderful performances in winning the World's Championship at Wimbledon more than a decade ago, but after her retirement America was forced to content itself with local honors.

Neither Miss Mary Browne nor Miss Hazel

Hotchkiss, now Mrs. George Wightman, followed
Mrs. May Sutton Bundy in her European invasion,
so the relative ability of our champions and Mrs.
Lambert-Chambers of England or Mlle. Brocadies
of France could not be judged. Mrs. Molla Bjurstedt Mallory followed Miss Browne as the outstanding figure in American tennis when the wonderful Norsewoman took the championship in 1915.
Miss Browne, then holder of the title, did not compete, so their relative ability could not be decided.
Throughout the period from 1900 to 1919 the
woman's championship event had been held annually
in June.   The result was that the blue ribbon event
was over so early in the season that the incentive for
play during July and August died a natural death.

   Finally in 1920, at the request of the Women's
Committee, particularly on the advice of Mrs.
George Wightman, the national champion, and Miss
Florence Ballin of New York, under whose able
guidance the entire schedule was drawn up, the
United States Lawn Tennis Association moved the
Women's Championship to September. Miss Ballin,
following the successful system used in the men's
events, organized a schedule that paralleled the big
fixtures on the men's schedule and placed in operation "a circuit," as it is called, that provided for
tournaments weekly from May to September. Miss
Ballin, together with Mrs. Wightman, organised
Junior tournaments for girls under 18, along the
lines used for the boys' events. The response was
immediate. Entry lists, which in the old days were

in "the teens," jumped to the thirties or forties, in the regular events. Young girls who, up to now, had not played tournaments, fearing they lacked the necessary class, rushed to play in the Junior girls' events. From this latter class came such a promising young star of today as Miss Martha Bayard, who bids fair to be national champion at some not distant date.

It was a tremendous task of organization that Miss Ballin and her assistants undertook, but they did it in a most efficient manner. Mrs. Molla Bjurstedt Mallory lent her invaluable assistance by playing in as many tournaments as possible. She was a magnet that drew the other players in her wake with an irresistible force.

1920 saw Mrs. Mallory's first invasion of Europe since her American triumphs. Misfortune was her portion. She was ill before sailing and, never at her best on shipboard, a bad voyage completed the wreck of her condition. She had little time for practice in England and it was a player far below her best who went down to crushing defeat at the hands of Mrs. Lambert-Chambers in the semifinal round of the World's Championship at Wimbledon.

Defeated but not discouraged, Mrs. Mallory returned to America and, again reaching her true form, won the championship with ease. She made up her mind the day of her defeat in England that 1921 would again find her on European courts.

The season of 1921 in America opened in a blaze

of tournaments throughout the entire country. Mrs. Mallory showed early in the year she was at her best by winning the Indoor Championship of the United States from one of the most representative fields ever gathered together for this event.

Early May found Mrs. Mallory on the seas bound for France and England. The story of her magnificent, if losing, struggle in both countries is told elsewhere in this book, but she sailed for home recognised abroad as one of the great players of the world, a thing which many of the foreign critics had not acknowledged the previous year.

The trip of the American team to France, and particularly the presence of Mrs. Mallory, coupled with the efforts of the Committee for Devastated France, finally induced Mlle. Suzanne Lenglen, the famous French World's Champion, to consent to come to America. The announcement of her decision started a boom in the game that has been un-equalled. Out in California, Mrs. May Sutton Bundy and Miss Mary Kendall Browne, our former champions, heard the challenge and, laying aside the duties of everyday life, buckled on the armour of the courts and journeyed East to do battle with the French wonder girl. Mrs. Mallory, filled with a desire to avenge her defeat in France, sailed for home in time to play in the American championship.

What a marvelous tournament this proved to be! In very truth it was a World's Championship. Mrs. May Sutton Bundy, former world's champion, back again after fifteen years with all her old charm of

manner, much of her speed of shot and foot, and
even more cunning and experience; Miss Mary K.
Browne, brilliant, fascinating, clever Mary, with all
her old-time personality and game that three times
had carried her to the highest honors in American
tennis; Mrs. Mallory, keen, determined and re-
sourceful, defending the title she had held so long
and well; the young players, rising in the game, struggling to attain the heights, and finally looming over
all the figure of the famous French champion of
champions, Suzanne Lenglen, considered by many
competent critics the greatest woman tennis player
of all time.

The stage was set for the sensational, and for
once it occurred. The God of Luck took a hand in
the blind draw and this resulted in all the stars,
with the exception of Miss Mary Browne, falling in
one half. Mlle. Suzanne Lenglen was drawn against
Miss Eleanor Goss, while Mrs. Mallory met Mrs.
Marion Zinderstein Jessop, her famous rival, in
the first round, with the winners of these matches
to play each other in the second.

Unfortunately illness prevented Mlle. Lenglen
from sailing at her appointed time. She arrived in
America but one day before the tournament was to
start. The officials of the United States Lawn Tennis Association wisely granted Mlle. Lenglen another day's grace by holding her match with Miss
Goss until Tuesday. Mrs. Mallory, playing brilliantly, crushed Mrs. Jessop on Monday.

Then came the deluge! Miss Goss, taken sud-

denly ill, was forced to default to Mlle. Lenglen
on Tuesday and Mrs. Mallory was called upon to
meet the great French player in Mlle. Lenglen's
first American appearance.

There is no question but what it was a terribly
hard position for Mlle. Lenglen. Mrs. Mallory was
physically and mentally on the crest. She had lived
for this chance ever since Mlle. Lenglen had defeated her at St. Cloud in June. Now it was hers
and she determined to make the most of it.

The two women stepped on the court together.
Mlle. Lenglen was obviously and naturally nervous.
Mrs. Mallory was quietly, grimly confident. Her
whole attitude said "I won't be beaten." Every one
of the 10,000 spectators felt it and joined with her
in her determination. It was an electric current between the gallery and the player. I felt it and am
sure that Mlle. Lenglen must have done so too. It
could not fail to impress her. The match opened
with Mrs. Mallory serving. From the first ball,
the American champion was supreme. Such tennis
I have never seen and I verily believe it will never
be seen again. The French girl was playing well.
She was as good as when she defeated Mrs. Mallory
in France or Miss Ryan in England, but this time
she was playing a super-woman who would not miss.
One cannot wonder her nerves, naturally over-
wrought, broke under the strain.

Mrs. Mallory, in an exhibition of faultless, flaw-
less tennis, ran through the first set 6–2. It was at
this point Mlle. Lenglen made her mistake.

She had trouble getting her breath and was obviously feeling the strain of her tremendous exertions. She defaulted the match! Mrs. Mallory walked from the court conqueror, clearly the superior of the much vaunted world's champion.

It is regrettable Mlle. Lenglen defaulted, for if she had played out the match, everyone would have made full allowance for her defeat, due, it would be said, to natural reaction from her recent sea journey. No one would have been quicker to make allowance for Mlle. Lenglen than Mrs. Mallory herself. The whole tennis public deeply regretted an incident that might well have been avoided.

Mrs. Mallory was the woman of the hour. She marched on to victory and successfully defended her title by virtue of victories over Mrs. May Sutton Bundy in the semi-final and Miss Mary Browne in the final.

Marvellous Molla! World's Champion in 1921 beyond shadow of dispute!

It is deplorable that the quite natural reaction and nervous upset, coupled with a return of her bronchial illness, forced Mlle. Lenglen to return to France before she was able to play her exhibition tour for the Committee for Devastated France. Possibly 1922 will find conditions more favorable and the Gods of Fate will smile on the return of Mlle. Lenglen to America.

(Molla Bjurstedt)

One of the most remarkable personalities in the tennis world is Mrs. Molla Bjurstedt Mallory, the American Champion and actually Champion of the World, 1921.

Mrs. Mallory is a Norsewoman by birth. She came to America in 1915. In 1919 she married Franklin I. Mallory, and thus became an American citizen.

It is a remarkable game which Mrs. Mallory has developed. She has no service of real value. Her overhead is nil, her volleying is mediocre; but her marvellous forehand and backhand drives, coupled with the wonderful court-covering ability and fighting spirit that have made her world-famous, allow her to rise above the inherent weaknesses of those portions of her game and defeat in one season all the greatest players in the world, including Mlle. Suzanne Lenglen.

Mrs. Mallory, with delightful smile, never failing sportsmanship and generosity in victory or defeat, is one of the most popular figures in tennis.

MRS. THOMAS C. BUNDY
(May Sutton)

It is said "they never come back," but Mrs. May Sutton Bundy has proved that at least one

MRS. FRANKLIN I. MALLORY [MOLLA BJURSTEDT]
America

MRS. MARION ZINDORSTEIN JESSUP
America

MISS MARY K. BROWNE
America

MLLE. LENGLEN
France

MISS ELIZABETH RYAN
America

MRS. MAY SUTTON BUNDY
America

MRS. LARCOMBE AND
MRS. LAMBERT CHAMBERS
British Isles

great athlete is an exception to the saying. Fifteen years ago, May Sutton ruled supreme among the women tennis stars of the world.

In 1921 Mrs. May Sutton Bundy, mother of four children, after a retirement of over a decade, returned to the game when Mlle. Lenglen announced her intention of invading America. If Mlle. Lenglen's visit to our shores did nothing more than bring Mrs. Bundy and Miss Browne back to us, it was well worth while.

Mrs. Bundy in 1921 was still a great player. She has a peculiar reverse twist service, a wonderful forehand drive, but with excessive top spin, a queer backhand poke, a fine volley and a reliable overhead. Much of her old aggressiveness and speed of foot are still hers. She retains all of her famous fighting spirit and determination, while she is even more charming and delightful than of old. She is a remarkable woman, who stands for all that is best in the game.

MARY KENDALL BROWNE

The return of another former National Champion in 1921 in the person of Mary K. Browne, who held the title in 1912, '13 and '14, brought us again a popular idol. The tennis public has missed Miss Browne since 1914 and her return was in the nature of a personal triumph.

Mary Browne has the best produced tennis game of any American woman. It is almost if not quite the equal in stroke technique of Suzanne Lenglen. She has a fast flat service. Her ground strokes are clean, flat drives forehand and backhand. She volleys exactly like Billy Johnston. No praise can be higher. Her overhead is decisive but erratic. She couples this beautiful game with a remarkable tennis head and a wonderful fighting spirit.

Miss Browne is a trig and trim little figure on the court as she glides over its surface. It is no wonder that her public love her.

MRS. GEORGE WIGHTMAN
(Hazel Hotchkiss)

The woman to whom American tennis owes its greatest debt in development is Hazel Hotchkiss Wightman, National Champion 1909, '10, '11 and 1919. Mrs. Wightman has practically retired from singles play. Her decision cost the game a wonderful player. She has a well placed slice service, a ground game that is essentially a chop fore- and backhand, although at times she drives off her forehand. She volleys remarkably. She is the equal of Mary Browne in this department, while her overhead is the best of any woman in the game.

Hazel Wightman is as clever a court general and tactician, man or woman, as I have ever known. She has forgotten more tennis than most of us ever learn. She is the Norman Brookes of woman's tennis.

It is not only in her game that Mrs. Wightman

has stood for the best in tennis, but she has given freely of her time and ability to aid young players in the game. She made Marion Zinderstein Jessop the fine player she is. Mrs. Wrightman is always willing to offer sound advice to any player who desires it.

Mrs. Wightman and Miss Florence Ballin are the prime factors in the new organization of woman's tennis that has resulted in the great growth of the game in the past two years.

MRS. JESSOP
(Marion Zinderstein)

There is no player in tennis of greater promise than Marion Zinderstein Jessop. She has youth, a wonderful game, the result of a sound foundation given her by Hazel Wightman, and a remarkable amount of experience for so young a girl. She has a beautiful fast service, but erratic. Her ground-game is perfectly balanced, as she chops or drives from either side with equal facility. She volleys with great severity and certainty. Her overhead is possibly her weakest point. She lacks the confidence that her game really deserves.

HELEN WILLS

The most remarkable figure that has appeared on the horizon of woman's tennis since Suzanne Lenglen first flashed into the public eye, is little Helen Wills of California, Junior Champion of

1921. She is only fifteen. Stocky, almost ungainly, owing to poor footwork, her hair in pigtails down her back, she is a quaint little person who instantly walks into hearts of the gallery.

The tennis this child plays is phenomenal. She serves with the power and accuracy of a boy. She drives and chops forehand and backhand with reckless abandon. She rushes to the net and kills in a way that is reminiscent of Maurice McLoughlin. Suddenly she dubs the easiest sort of a shot and grins a happy grin. There is no doubt she is already a great player. She should become much greater. She is a miniature Hazel Wightman in her game. Above all, she is that remarkable combination, an unspoiled child and a personality.

There are many other players of real promise coming to the front. Boston boasts of a group that contains Mrs. Benjamin E. Cole (Anne Sheafe) who has made a great record in the season of 1921; Miss Edith Sigourney, who accompanied Mrs. Mallory abroad, Miss Leslie Bancroft and Mrs. Godfree. There are Miss Martha Bayard, Miss Helen Gilleandean, Mrs. Helene Pollak Folk, Miss Molly Thayer, Miss Phyllis Walsh and Miss Anne Townsend in New York and Philadelphia.

France
MLLE. SUZANNE LENGLEN

There is no more unique personality, nor more remarkable player among the women than Mademoiselle Suzanne Lenglen, the famous French girl who holds the World's Championship title. Mlle. Lenglen is a remarkable figure in the sporting world. She has personality, individuality, and magnetism that hold the public interest. She is the biggest drawing card in the tennis world.

Mlle. Lenglen's fame rests on her drive. Strange though it may seem, her drive is the least interesting part of her game. Mlle. Lenglen uses a severe overhead service of good speed. It is a remarkable service for a woman, one which many men might do well to copy. Her famous forehand drive is a full arm swing from the shoulder. It meets the ball just as Mlle. Lenglen springs in the air. The result is pictorially unique, but not good tennis. She loses speed and power by this freak. Her backhand is beautifully played, from perfect footwork, with a free swing and topped drive. It is a remarkable stroke. Her volleying is perfect in execution and result. She hits her overhead smash freely with a "punch" that is as great as many men. It is as fine an overhead as that of Mrs. George Wightman, the American Champion.

Mlle. Lenglen's speed of foot is marvellous. She runs fast and easily. She delights in acrobatic jumps, many of them unnecessary, at all times during her play. She is a wonderful gallery player, and wins the popularity that her dashing style deserves. She is a brilliant court general, conducting her attack with a keen eye on both the court and the gallery.

Mlle. Lenglen is not outstanding among the women players of the world, in my opinion. She is probably the best stroke player in the world to-day, yet Mrs. Lambert Chambers, Mrs. George Wightman, Miss Elizabeth Ryan, Mrs. Franklin L. Mallory (formerly Miss Molla Bjurstedt), Miss Mary Browne, and Mrs. May Sutton Bundy are all in her class in match play. There is no woman playing tennis that has the powerful personality of Mlle. Lenglen. Her acrobatic style and grace on the court form an appeal no gallery can resist. Her very mannerisms fool people into considering her far greater than she really is, even though she is a wonderful player.

MME. BILLOUTT
(Mlle. Brocadies)

Second only to Suzanne Lenglen in France is Mme. Billoutt, formerly Mlle. Brocadies, once the idol of the Paris tennis public. This remarkable player has as perfectly developed a game as I have seen. Her actual stroking is the equal of Mlle. Lenglen. Her strokes are all orthodox, flat racquet ones. Her ground game is based wholly on the drive, fore- or backhand. She has grown rather heavier in the last few years and consequently slowed up, but she is still one of the great players of the world.

England

In marked contrast to the eccentricities of Mlle. Lenglen one finds the delightfully polished style of Mrs. Lambert Chambers. Mrs. Chambers has a purely orthodox game of careful execution that any student of the game should recognize as the highest form of tennis strokes.

Mrs. Chambers serves an overhead delivery of no particular movement. She slices or "spoons" her ground strokes, forehand or backhand. She seldom volleys or smashes. Her only excursions to the net are when she is drawn to the net.

It is not Mrs. Chambers' game itself so much as what she does with it, that I commend so highly. Her change of pace and distance is wonderfully controlled. Her accuracy marvellous. Her judgment is remarkable, and the way in which she saves undue exertion is an art in itself. She gets a wonderful return for her outlay of effort.

Hers is a personality of negation. Her manner on the court is negative, her shots alone are positive. She is never flustered, and rarely shows emotion.

Mrs. Chambers is the "Mavro" of women as regards her recovering ability. Her errors are reduced to a minimum at all times. To err is human; but at times there is something very nearly inhuman about Mrs. Chambers' tennis.

ELIZABETH RYAN

The English-American star Elizabeth Ryan is another player of marked individuality. Born in California, Miss Ryan migrated to England while quite young. For the past decade "Bunny," as she is called, has been a prominent figure in English and Continental tournaments.

Miss Ryan has a queer push-reverse twist service that is well placed but carries little speed. She chops viciously forehand and backhand off the ground and storms the net at every opening. Her volleying is crisp and decisive. Overhead she is severe but erratic. She is a dogged fighter, never so dangerous as when behind. Her tactics are aggressive attack at all times, and if this fails she is lost.

Although Miss Ryan is an American by birth she must be considered as an English player, for her development is due to her play in England.

MRS. BEAMISH

This English player is an exponent of the famous base-line game of the country. She drives, long deep shots fore- and backhand, corner to corner, chasing her opponent around the court almost impossible distances. Her service volleying and overhead are fair but not noteworthy. Another player of almost identical game and of almost equal class is Mrs. Peacock, Champion of India. Her whole game is a little better rounded than Mrs. Beamish, but she lacks the latter's experience.

Among the other women in England who are delightfully original in their games are Mrs. Larcombe, the wonderful chop-stroke player, whose clever generalship and tactics place her in the front rank, and Mrs. M'Nair, with her volleying attack.

Women's tennis in England is on a slightly higher plane at this time than in America; but the standard of play in America is rapidly coming up. International competition between women on the lines of the Davis Cup, for which a trophy has previously been offered by Lady Wavertree in England, and in 1919 by Mrs. Wightman in America, and twice refused by the International Federation, would do more than any other factor to place women's tennis on the high plane desired. This plan has succeeded for the men, why should it not do as well for the women?